To Anne,

Enjoy Lizzie Journey to Freedom!

Lizzie's Story: A Slave Family's Journey to Freedom

By

Clarice Boswell

Dr. Clarice Boswell

ISBN: 978-0-7596-9920-5 (sc)
ISBN: 978-1-4033-3290-5 (hc)
ISBN: 978-0-7596-9919-9 (e)

Print information available on the last page.

This book is printed on acid-free paper.

1st Books - rev. 10/11/22

Dedications:

Thanks to my husband, Henry, and children Constance, Claudia, Cathy, and Christopher, whose encouragement sustained me during the writing of this book, and for John and Frank, Jr., my two brothers, whose faith in me helped make the book a reality.

In loving memory of Mama Lizzie, my grandmother, and my parents, Frank Robert and Ora Belle Cannon.

Acknowledgements

John M. Cannon, my younger brother in Seattle, Washington, for the endless hours he spent typing, critiquing and formatting the book for publication. Without his encouragement and patience, this journey would have been impossible. Henry A. Boswell, my soul mate since 1957, for his persistence and endless hours of carefully reading draft after draft of this book. Frank R. Cannon, Jr., my older brother, for his enthusiasm and willingness to help research the archives for pertinent history that enhanced the authenticity of this book. Constance L. (Boswell) Martin, Claudia L. (Boswell) Ellis, Cathy L. Boswell, and Christopher L. Boswell, my children, who followed the journey from its beginning. I leave them a legacy to cherish for generations to come. I am thankful for their support and willingness to help critique and enhance the contents of this book.

I would also like to acknowledge my debt to Hubert "Ruby" Boswell, my 97-year-old father-in-law, who has always been a source of support and inspiration to me. First cousins Horace Patrick and Joyce (Patrick) Morlin, they shared the stories that their mother told them about the family. Also Nancy Grider, retired English teacher from Joliet, for help on editing of this book.

Also Louise (Black) Poindexter and Mary L. Martin, my only two remaining aunts, will always be remembered for their encouraging words and support of this book. I am also indebted to my graphic artist Eric Hines for his time and talent in designing the cover. The pictures used to design the cover represent the authentic rocking chair, the 1876 family Bible, and patch quilt quilted by Mama. There are numerous local residents that have encouraged me daily to complete the book. To those sources I owe a debt of thanks including the Sisters of the Joliet Area Alumni Chapter, Delta Sigma Theta Sorority, Inc., and the members of Grace United Methodist Church, Joliet, Illinois.

To those whose contributions I have neglected to mention, please accept my sincere apology. I owe all a great debt.

Table of Contents

Prologue

This is a story of an African family that arrived in America from West Africa on a slave merchant ship in the spring of 1850. Upon arriving in Maryland through the Chesapeake Bay they were placed in a holding stockade in Annapolis, which was among the smallest auction markets for slaves destined for the states of Kentucky, Tennessee, and Alabama. The family had survived the three-month Middle Passage journey across the Atlantic Ocean only to be auctioned to the highest plantation slave broker bid. The family consisted of mother, father, and two children ages five and seven.

Although the families are fact, some of the names and background information are fictional. Most of the factual information was gathered from family members, the 1876 family Bible, and information from many documented family pictures dating back to 1854. The old family Bible and photo albums enabled the writer to connect and envision the spirit of a family that encountered undue hardship, and physical and mental treatment that was harsh and cruel.

In creating the background for the story, the writer drew on much of the first-person dialogue to document actual accounts of events that the family encountered upon arriving in America in 1850.

As late as 1850 in some coastal areas along the Atlantic, the slave laws continued to be enforced as the need for free labor proved economically profitable. Federal laws, restricting slavery seemed useless, as they were ignored by white masters, politicians, and others who were slave owners.

Slave brokers, acting as sellers in the north and buyers in the south, were licensed traders who bought and sold slaves on speculation. Delcy's parents, Eli and Leah Brent, and her two brothers, Josh and Reuben, were all auctioned and imprisoned in a stockade storage in Annapolis, Maryland. It is, however, a known fact that they arrived at the market house in Annapolis Harbor, Maryland as a family destined for slavery. This was a relatively small holding port because foreign slave trade had been greatly reduced since most states were purchasing slaves from the domestic market.

Slaves who were purchased for Kentucky plantations made an overland trip on foot across the mountains to reach their destination. Often at night they would sleep in jails, churches or warehouses. To ensure safe arrival, the human cargo was always chained and shackled.

Lizzie Brent Sheff Davis Cannon, born December 25, 1870, was the mother of eight children and one foster daughter, Katherine Louise Black, whom she raised from the age of five. At Lizzie's death on September 8, 1965, at the age of 94, she had nine grand children and four children living that lovingly called her Mama.

The map follows the route the Brent family traveled from Maryland to Kentucky. Eli and Leah Brent and their two sons, Josh and Reuben, landed on the shore of America in the spring of 1850. They were auctioned from the slave-holding pens at Annapolis, Maryland to a tobacco plantation master in Kentucky. With the aid of a slave broker representing Master Sheff, the difficult journey by foot

from Maryland into West Virginia and finally into Kentucky took about seven weeks. They were chained together and allowed to rest only a few times a day at which time they shared a few pieces of bread and drink of water. At night they slept in abandoned buildings or jails that provided rooms for traveling slaves. The journey ended in Leesburg, Kentucky at the plantation of Lloyd and Sarah Sheff, who would prove to be ruthless and cruel owners.

CHAPTER 1—1850: FROM AFRICA TO MARYLAND, THE LONGEST JOURNEY

The year 1850 was filled with devastating slave laws that tightened the screws of bondage on the institution of slavery in America. The Fugitive Slave Law of 1850 allowed bounty hunters to capture slaves in any state of the Union regardless of their status as a fugitive or free person and return them to their owners or re-sell them into slavery. Because the slaves were in a majority in most states, the labor market for illegally transporting Africans across the Atlantic to be auctioned and sold into slavery was no longer necessary.

When the Eli and Leah Brent family was captured from Africa and forced on the slave ship bound for America, they were among the last Africans to illegally cross the Atlantic. The 3-month journey was terrifying and very difficult. There was fear, hatred, and confusion among the slaves. Shackled to the floor, the slaves were beaten and denied food and water by the slave brokers. Many slave taskmasters used a dialect unfamiliar to the slaves, thus increasing an even greater fear for the Africans.

Many Africans did not survive the seemingly endless journey because of cruelty, starvation, and disease. Even though the slave brokers always chose the strongest and healthiest slaves they thought would survive the journey, they did not consider the possibility of the slaves contracting illnesses that were common in America but fatal in their African homeland. Nor did they count on having very strong willed, rebellious Africans who would rather jump ship and drown than become a slave.

Eli and Leah watched with horror throughout the entire journey many deaths and suicides. They tried to keep Josh and Reuben's eyes away from such terrifying deaths, but they couldn't protect their children from all of the nightmares. On this particular voyage more than a fourth of the cargo did not arrive at its final destination. The slave brokers were not happy with the fact that so many died on the voyage, for they lost money.

The Brent family huddled tightly in a corner of the hold of the ship (bottom, where the rats were) and prayed they would make it safely to their destination. Little did they know the hardships of disease, pain, and death that awaited their arrival in America. Upon landing in Annapolis, Maryland the Brent family was removed from the ship's cargo bay and placed in a holding stockade. Here they would remain until it was time for them to be placed on the auction block and sold to the highest bidder.

Eli attempted to comfort his family as he spoke softly to his wife Leah,

"Leah, everything is going to be all right, you hear? You just hold on to me and the boys real tight. We're going to be all right."

The two sons, Reuben, age 7, and Josh, age 5, trembled with fear as they clung to their parents. Their greatest fear was being separated and never seeing Mama Leah and Papa Eli again. Eli drew his family close to his body. He knew they were cold from the damp floor in the holding pen. He was a big, strong man standing over six feet tall, with deep, piercing eyes and high cheekbones. His rich brown complexion was representative of the native African arriving in America.

Leah and Eli comforted each other and the two boys as the family was harshly steered toward the auction steps. They witnessed other families weeping and clinging to each other as they were separated and sold to the highest bidder. Eli whispered to Leah,

"For some reason, they are keeping us together as a family." Leah breathed a sigh of relief.

Prior to the start of the auction, Zac Wallace, the slave broker, had an opportunity to discuss with the auctioneer his intent to purchase a family unit for Lloyd Sheff's tobacco plantation. Because Zac was a frequent buyer for the southern slave owners, he felt that the auctioneer would attempt to honor his request.

The auctioneer started the bid at $500 for the family. Eli felt humiliated when they stripped him of his clothes and examined his body for form and physical stature. Leah was spared the fate of many younger women whom she observed being stripped and humiliated.

Zac Wallace watched the bidders around him shouting out bids on Eli, while mostly ignoring Leah and the two boys. Zac could see the family being split by individual bids. Lloyd Sheff had given strict orders for Zac to purchase a complete family of slaves of good health and robust stature to work on his tobacco plantation in Leesburg, Ky. Zac became fearful of losing the opportunity to secure the family as the bidding continued to climb on Eli.

Suddenly, the bid was fifteen hundred dollars for Eli with only a few meager bids for Leah and the two boys. Zac could see the deal slipping away. Lloyd Sheff had entrusted him with three thousand dollars to bid on a family. Suddenly Zac yelled out,

"I bid twenty eight hundred dollars on the whole family."

Immediately, a murmur came over the crowd but no other bids were forthcoming. A few tense moments elapsed and the auctioneer shouted, "Going once, going twice, sold to the gentleman from Kentucky!" The auctioneer instructed the recorder of sales to document the purchase of the Brent family consisting of one male named Eli, age 26, one female named Leah, age 24, and two small boys, Reuben, age 7, and Josh, age 5.

Eli loved his family and in his own way, he quietly expressed thankfulness that his family was not separated. After the sale was recorded, not much time lapsed before Zac prepared the family for the journey to the Sheff's tobacco plantation. Eli, Leah, Reuben, and Josh were huddled together awaiting instructions from Zac. They were poorly dressed for the cold long journey. Zac rode his prancing stallion as the family struggled to keep up on foot. The children tired more quickly since there was very little food and water to spare during the long journey.

At one point, Josh began to cry, as it was hard for him to keep pace. Reuben picked Josh up and put him on his back.

"Don't cry, Josh." Reuben consoled.

"You ain't heavy. Wrap yo' legs around me and hol' on tight."

Josh was also getting hungry, but he didn't dare ask for anything. Zac had a terrible temper that scared the boys. When they had trouble keeping up, Zac would harshly scold them. Once he even snapped his whip as a warning for everyone to keep up. Eli and Leah were chained together and the boys walked beside them. The journey was rugged and the terrain up and down the hills was difficult for everyone. Leah would gently nudge the boys when she noticed they were lagging behind. Zac had a deadline to deliver the Brent family to Lloyd by the last of May in time to start planting tobacco.

Reuben and Josh often spoke quietly to each other. They were so afraid of what might happen to them. Josh confided in Reuben,

"Reuben, do you think they will take us away from Mama and Papa?"

"I don't think so Josh, but if they wanted to, they would have done that when Papa was standing on the steps and everyone was looking at him."

"Reuben?"

"Yeah Josh?"

"Mama looked so scared."

"Yeah, Josh."

"The other children were crying. It made me cry."

"Reuben?"

"Yeah, Josh."

"Where are we going?"

"I ain't sure, Josh, it's a long way from home." "Reuben? I miss home. Will we ever get to go back?"

"I ain't sure Josh."

"Reuben, I'm thirsty and I know Mama and Papa must be too."

The sun was beginning to go down and the evening's cool was causing Eli, Leah, and the two boys to shiver. All of them were extremely tired as they wearily moved forward, hoping that they would soon stop. Zac seemed to sense the exhaustion of the family and soon stopped at a nearby jail where food and shelter were provided the family. Day after day passed, seemingly endless: Maryland, West Virginia, and finally into Kentucky. Tired, weary, with blisters on their feet, and clothes tattered, they pushed forward on their journey.

The need for slave labor on the tobacco plantations was crucial during the 1850's. The demand for exporting tobacco made very profitable business. Cotton in the South, along with sugar, rice, and hemp, was expanding the demand for slave labor. The closer the family got to the plantation, the harder Zac drove them. However, during the last few days of the journey, he made certain they had an ample portion of food and water. It was essential that Zac Wallace deliver the family in good physical condition. After more than six weeks, the Brent family arrived on the plantation in Leesburg, Ky, where Master Lloyd and Miss Sarah impatiently awaited their delivery.

The slave taskmaster, Boss Calhoun, showed the family to their living quarters. The old, run-down log cabin located closer to the fields than to the master's house was in serious need of repair. Inside the one-room cabin was a potbellied stove, a pecan wood rocking chair, a bed, a table and four chairs, and a kerosene lamp. This was all very strange to the Brent family, because in Africa, not only were the

6

structure and furnishings different, but the village style of living where everyone supported each other as neighbors no longer existed. In Africa, the huts were made of bamboo and mud. Inside, covering the ground, were decorative and durable rugs that served as beds for the family. The tribal style of living was open and uninhibited. Men, women, and children were free to move about in social gatherings. Meals were prepared outside of the hut by the women in the village. The meal was a time for family unity and celebrating the collaborative efforts of the village people to have food as well as friendship.

As the Brent family huddled in their new home in America, fear rushed over them. They were in a strange land, with a strange language, and no familiar faces. Josh and Reuben were curious about the children who stared at them, saying nothing. Pearlie, their neighbor next door, was just as curious. Now she knew why Master Lloyd had sold the Weaver family in the log cabin next to her. It was to make room for a younger family.

After a few hours, Pearlie, the neighbor next door, gently knocked on the Brent's door. She was well groomed in a long gray dress and crisp starched apron that covered her shoes. The family stared with fear not knowing what to expect. The journey for the Brent family had been long and tiring, and no one had shown any acts of kindness toward them. Suddenly, Pearlie's face broke into a big smile and she extended a hand to Eli and Leah. She had prepared a pot of stew to welcome them to the life of slavery. She motioned for the family to sit down while she found a few things upon which to serve the food. The family was very hungry, especially the children.

Pearlie made many visits to the new family next door. During these visits, she began to develop various hand and body gestures accompanied by words as a means of communicating with the family, especially Leah. They began to bond as they walked to and from work. Several months later, as the family began to understand and relate to Pearlie, she told them about overhearing Master Lloyd negotiating with Zac Wallace to ride out to Annapolis, Maryland and bid on a family that he had an inside track on that was arriving on a merchant ship in April 1850. Pearlie knew she could use the help in the Master's house. After all, the Sheff children and the whims of Miss Sarah were a full time morning-till-night job and often overwhelming.

It was late May when the Sheff plantation owner took delivery of the Brent family. Pearlie was beginning to put together the idea of what Master Lloyd and Miss Sarah were thinking when they sold the Weaver family in the end cabin. Clifton and Bernice Weaver had been on the plantation for nearly twenty years. Fannie, their 17-year old daughter, had a rough time working in the fields. She wanted so much to work in the main house, but she knew that as long as Pearlie was there she would always be a field hand. Two of their sons, Morie, age 19, and James, age 21, had fled through the Underground Railroad and Master Lloyd knew it was only a matter of time before their third son Ralph, age 23, would join his brothers. Master Lloyd wanted a younger family that could grow up on the plantation as the Weaver family had.

Pearlie valued the Brent family, and in her spare time she let them know that the life of a slave was harsh and bitter. She told them how to stay out of the way of the overseer's whip, and what to expect from Miss Sarah. The family listened carefully as they slowly adjusted to the life of a slave with no rights or privileges that they once had in their homeland of Africa.

Leah was assigned to work in the main house with Pearlie. Miss Sarah was very impatient and resented showing Leah more than once how to do her job. Leah soon felt the harsh treatment of Miss Sarah. Leah did not have a good understanding of the English language, which made it even more difficult to adhere to Miss Sarah's demands. This lack of communication resulted in undue whipping and face slapping. Leah was very careful not to agitate or provoke Miss Sarah. She listened more carefully and soon began to understand more and more of what was expected of her. Quietly, she did her job, which consisted of cooking the meals, washing, ironing, making the beds, cleaning, and caring for Master Lloyd, Miss Sarah, and their three children. Pearlie comforted Leah when she returned home from the long day at Master Lloyd's house. Pearlie knew it was difficult to work for Miss Sarah. It was hard for Leah to keep up with the many demands of her own family as well.

Eli and the two boys were assigned to the tobacco fields under the supervision of Boss Calhoun, a very brutal man. Eli and the boys watched carefully the jobs of other slaves and soon became familiar with the tasks expected of slaves who worked the tobacco fields. Other slaves owned by Master Lloyd had huge scars on their backs which frightened Eli and the boys. They had never seen anything like those deep scars. No one on the plantation said much to each other. Head down with a strap over the shoulders harnessing a team of mules, they plowed and later planted from sunup to sundown. Afterward there was wood to cut and split and animals to care for.

After a few months with the help of Pearlie, Leah began to understand Miss Sarah better and especially to understand what was expected of slaves who worked in the master's house. For example, she learned how to please Miss Sarah when serving tea as well as presenting her with a new dress or a beautiful patch quilt made from scraps of fabric given her. Leah took no chances of feeling comfortable in Miss Sarah's presence. She could be just as ruthless as kind. Leah stayed on task and did her job well.

After a twelve or fourteen-hour day in the fields for Eli, Reuben and Josh, and a busy day at Master Lloyd's house for Leah, there were many things to do at the old broken down cabin. Seemingly, something always needed fixing. Eli remembered when the old roof was leaking on the mud floor. It made such a mess trying to dry out the beds. He had to put fresh straw on the floor to soak up the water. It was near fall before the old roof was fixed. He had to stuff mud between the logs to keep out the winter wind and snow.

After a long day at the Master's house, Leah had a meal to fix and sometimes water to carry from the well for her family. Leah would often do the mending and quilting after the two boys were asleep. On occasion, she would simply enjoy sitting in the old pecan rocking chair after she had carefully patched and mended the worn-out clothes. Most of the time the clothes had patches over patches.

Leah was always thinking about the family and trying to make life a bit more pleasant and comfortable. Sometimes she would surprise them with fresh straw mattresses or replace the worn out quilts with new ones made from discarded clothes from Master Lloyd's house.

Josh and Reuben were learning the routine of the plantation and took on more responsibilities. For example, every morning they had to hang the quilts on the fence to dry as a result of the dampness from the mud floor. Each day, they went to the fields with Eli and helped weed the crops as well as tend to the farm animals. Their evening chores were to make certain there was fresh water for the master's house. The boys hurried to finish the evening tasks so they could eat supper. They looked forward to Eli and Leah telling them stories about their life in Africa and the good old days, a life that they would never see again.

The daily demands on the Brent family seemed endless. They often talked about being free and wondered when freedom would become a reality. One day Eli asked another slave about the route to freedom and was told to never mention that again. The slave pointed to the scars on his back as a reminder of what to expect when slaves talked about freedom or the Northern Star. Eli became afraid for Leah, Reuben and Josh and warned them to never mention freedom to anyone. Eli believed that someday they would have a better life and be free, but had not yet allowed himself to make plans to improve their condition.

Eli and Leah sensed the tension on the plantation when Master Lloyd entertained visitors for dinner. Often Leah overheard the master talking about slaves running away and the awful things he threatened to do if he ever caught them on his plantation. Leah was often afraid for the fugitives who crossed the plantation late at night headed north. She cautiously gave them food and water and quickly sent them away.

As Leah sat in the old rocking chair, she often thought about the boys, now seven and nine years old. Each day the boys went to the tobacco field with Eli to help with the crops. Some days they were expected to pick vegetables from the garden and care for the farm animals. In the evening, they always made certain Leah had plenty wood for the fire that heated the water in the two big black pots in which she washed clothes. Reuben and Josh were obedient and well-behaved boys who did whatever was asked of them.

The boys loved the days when Leah sat in the rocking chair and Eli sat at the table smoking his corn cob pipe. He told them stories of life in their motherland of Africa. They liked to hear about the older boys in their village hunting and playing games where they could pretend to be great warriors. Sometimes the boys would look sad while longing for Africa where they were free to roam the countryside.

Eli always ended his stories,

"Those times all gone."

"Life will never be the same. Someday, if I live long enough, we shall be free."

12

Leah really missed her life in the village where activities were centered around families doing things together for the betterment of everyone. The village agricultural and trade market was the center of life for the family. The women would care for the gardens, weave the cloth, and tend the children. The older women would tell stories to the younger girls on the importance of the family, which formed the village. The women had a special way of preparing the girls for womanhood. They taught the young girls to work and instructed them about being a good mother. Leah remembered all they had said, and tried to practice the many things she had learned in her village.

Leah and Eli began to notice a number of runaway slaves crossing the fields down by the creek. They became very anxious for the boys. Boss Calhoun had warned all the slaves that they would get severe lashings with the whip if they were caught trying to escape. Eli wanted to protect the boys from escaping slaves who might try to persuade them to leave the plantation. The year was 1852, the demand for tobacco from the American and European market was at its highest for field workers. Adults and children worked from sun up until sun down.

Once when Master Lloyd was caught up on his work for a few days in the tobacco fields he decided to lease Eli out to another farmer. Other farmers were just as difficult to work for and often disallowed them the bare necessities, such as a drink of water. It was this type of cruelty that made slaves think about running for freedom. Eli thought, "where would he go? What would happen to him if he were caught? "Eli tried not to get too involved with the fugitive slaves. However, he longed to know what freedom would be like in America. Eli became afraid for himself and the boys. Reuben and Josh were warned to be careful when they saw escaping slaves. They always watched for Boss Calhoun and Master Lloyd. Eli realized that the boys could be sold for a high price at their age. The last thing Eli wanted was for his family to be sold as punishment for helping escaping slaves or talking about freedom.

CHAPTER 2—1854: PEARLIE

Pearlie was one of the most trusted slaves owned by Master Lloyd and Miss Sarah. She had arrived in America from the west coastal shore of Africa, having crossed the Atlantic on a merchant ship with her father, mother, and younger sister, all destined for Charleston, South Carolina in the year 1845. She had endured the harsh journey to America to be sold into a harsher situation. She saw many Africans die enroute to America. Often the stench and foul air in the hold of the ship was unbearable. There was barely room to turn and no room to sit or stand.

When Pearlie disembarked the merchant ship, she was placed in a holding pen along with her family and hundreds of other Africans waiting their turn to be stripped of their dignity, examined and auctioned like cattle to the highest bidder. She remembered well that hot, muggy day in Charleston when she was sexually fondled and stripped of her clothes and paraded up and down in front of the bidders for their approval.

Pearlie's father, mother, and younger sister were sold separately. Pearlie never saw them again. She often wondered what happened to them. Pearlie was auctioned to a tobacco plantation owner in Tennessee. She did not know the journey from Charleston to Tennessee would take six weeks on foot. She and two other slaves were purchased for the Shelby plantation. Pearlie was frequently sexually abused by the master and other white overseers from the moment she arrived on the Shelby plantation. One day she hemorrhaged so badly from the sexual assaults that she nearly died. After recovering, she found that she could never have children; thus, Pearlie was no longer a profitable slave. A barren slave was often useless, for slave owners expected pregnancies to ensure future slaves for profit.

Pearlie was put on the market again to be sold along with several other slaves from the Shelby plantation. Pearlie, now twenty, scared and helpless, was once again paraded in front of prospective buyers for a price. A slave broker representing Master Lloyd and Miss Sarah Sheff bid for her. Master Lloyd needed someone to help with the children. Pearlie was not worth as much as a barren slave woman but she would serve his household needs and she sold relatively cheap.

Miss Sarah took Pearlie into the master house and gave her the task of nurse and midwife for the family. Pearlie took her herbs and salves and nursed the Sheff family and nursed the slaves that had been whipped by the overseers for not pulling their weight on the plantation. Pearlie knew how to birth babies and care for the personal needs of Miss Sarah. When Miss Sarah was pregnant with her second baby, Pearlie was there to help with the delivery. Pearlie was by far Miss Sarah's most trusted house slave. After a few months, Master Lloyd provided a log cabin for Pearlie on the edge of the tobacco fields and she moved from the master's house. There were three cabins and an outhouse near the slave quarters. She liked that because she could see what was going on with the families that lived on either side. Periodically, the slave family on the other side of Pearlie would get together in the cabins and talk about freedom. Sometimes the women would swap stories about Master Lloyd and Miss Sarah. Pearlie would laugh about how she would listen to their stories and pretend not to understand. She said,

"I learned how to play along, always listening to their business."

Five years after Pearlie's arrival on the Sheff plantation, the Brent family moved into the cabin next to her. She would miss the Weaver family since they were working the tobacco fields when she was bought by Master Lloyd. Pearlie had watched the Weaver children grow up and escape from the plantation. Now, a younger family had taken their place.

Leah and Eli were grateful for the help of Pearlie. She was highly respected by the slaves for her status with the Sheff family. There were certain unspoken codes of discrimination based on the color of one's skin imposed on the slaves. Slaves that were assigned to work in the master's house had a higher status often causing resentment by those slaves assigned to work the fields. Pearlie was able to help the Brent family understand what was expected of them and how to survive the demands of the master and the social culture within the slave community.

CHAPTER 3—1854: DELCY

Four years after Leah, Eli, Josh and Reuben arrived in Leesburg, Kentucky, Leah reflected on the struggle that the family had gone through since arriving on the Sheff tobacco plantation. Reuben turned eleven in the fall and Josh, now nine, wanted more than anything to learn how to read and write. They would listen to the Sheff children read as Miss Sarah taught them daily. However, there was no alloted time for schooling of slaves on the plantation. In fact, the boys did not know any slaves that could read and write.

One day Eli had to take a trip off the plantation for Master Lloyd. He hooked up the team of mules to the old farm wagon and called to Reuben to hop on the seat beside him. Reuben was excited, for it was his first time ever off the plantation. Eli explained to him that they were going to the plantation down the road to pick up some seed for planting. Reuben had always wondered what was beyond the plantation. On the journey, he saw many beautiful horses and large mansions like Master Lloyd's. He also saw other slaves all dressed up with big top hats and red coats with bright shiny buttons driving carriages taking the master's mistress to and from town.

Eli warned Reuben to keep his head down so as not to imply anything between him and the beautiful mistresses all dressed up in silks and satins with beautiful hats and umbrellas. Reuben noticed that the fancily dressed slaves hopped off the carriage and opened the door to carefully help each passenger down. Those white women seemed happy. Their skin was pale and their hair was neatly curled with ribbons and bows. They were like nothing he had ever seen in his life. Eli saw the excitement in Reuben's eyes; he knew how much trouble a young, black, male slave could cause by looking at a white woman in a curious way.

Eli took this time to talk to Reuben. He told him how some slaves were punished, by either whipping or hanging, for just looking at a white woman. Reuben acknowledged everything Papa Eli told him. Getting in trouble was the last thing he wanted. Eli told him that he had heard of a young boy just like him being sold away from his mama and papa just for glancing at a mistress. Reuben stayed in the wagon while Eli loaded the seed in the back. Eli quickly stepped up on the wagon and gave the mules a snap as they hurriedly bumped their way back to the plantation. Reuben talked all the way home about the things he saw that day outside the plantation. He could hardly wait to tell Josh about his trip. Josh was full of questions and anxious to hear about everything that Reuben had seen.

Josh and Reuben were beginning to ask questions about the life of other people beyond the plantation. Their curiosity grew more each day as they saw the runaway slaves in the evenings after all the field bosses were gone. They became brave and discretely asked a few slaves which way they were headed. They knew they were seeking freedom because Papa and Mama Leah had slipped the fugitive slaves food through the kitchen window and sent them on their way. The boys eventually put together bits and pieces of information and started to understand that thing called, "The Underground Railroad," would take them North toward freedom. Leah decided it was the right time to talk to the boys about the things she had heard from Pearlie. The Master's guests talked about the escaping slaves and the Underground Railroad. Seemingly, the Masters did not know how so many slaves were finding their way North.

Pearlie had observed the same curiosity and desire for freedom in Josh and Reuben as she did in the Weaver boys. They escaped the Sheff plantation prior to the arrival of the Brent family. Pearlie became increasingly concerned for the safety of the boys and decided to share with Leah the secret codes of the quilts used by the fugitive slaves to make their journey north.

Although Pearlie had seen many fugitive slaves crossing the Sheff plantation, she did not share her knowledge of the codes, patterns, and hidden secrets of the quilts. She knew that information would let the slaves know where they could stop for food and shelter on "The Liberty Trail," later known as the Underground Railroad. She explained to Leah that the Underground Railroad was a secret group of people who cared about freeing slaves by helping them escape; by letting them use their homes for shelter, fixing them food, giving them clothes and medicines, and even showing them the way to the next safe place. Some of the secret people were called abolitionists. They helped hide and direct the slaves by developing the carefully selected patterns in the quilts that contained the messages and maps.

The abolitionists would visit the different plantations pretending to be merchants peddling house wares, tax collectors or census takers. They knew the blacksmith was the trusted servant in many instances. Pearlie knew Pete, the blacksmith, from the Shelby plantation in

Tennessee. She knew Pete had contact with almost everyone entering the Shelby plantation. Knowing that Pearlie was a quilter, he asked her to make several quilts using the special patterns that had been shown to him by the abolitionists.

Pearlie had witnessed slaves severely punished by her past master. She knew Master Lloyd would deal out the same punishment to his slaves who offered help to fugitives crossing his plantation. It was with the greatest of confidence and promise of secrecy that Pete shared the messages with Pearlie which she now shared with Leah.

She continued to explain to Leah that the simple quilt was one item that was common to both the master's and the slave's household.

Leah learned from Pearlie that the grandmother's flower garden quilt indicated that there was a root cellar or shed with a false floor to hide under behind the flower garden. This really impressed Leah. Pearlie told Leah how she was entrusted with the quilt codes while working on the Shelby plantation.

Leah carefully explained to her sons how secret codes were hidden in the quilts as a message to help the runaway slaves find safe houses on their way north to freedom. The Sheff plantation was not a safe stop for runaway slaves. However, every chance Leah got, she would share a piece of bread or drink of water, always hoping she would not get caught.

Leah really wanted the boys to know the danger of escaping, the danger of not knowing what to expect beyond the plantation, and most of all, danger of not knowing who could be trusted. There were many dangers in escaping, especially alone. The Masters had well-trained dogs that would hunt a slave down. If the slave did not know which direction to go, they could be easily tracked, found, and re-sold. Being sold away from one's parents was just one of the punishments for running. The boys thought long and hard about the possibility of being separated from Papa and Mama Leah.

One night when all was quiet and the old fire in the cooking stove was cooling down there was a tap at the kitchen window. It scared everyone. Papa Eli asked the family to stay quiet. He moved slowly toward the door and asked,

"Who is it?" A soft, quiet voice spoke,

"A friend, who just wants a little food and a drink of water."

Leah moved quietly around the cabin, filling a small cloth sack with a few leftover biscuits and a piece of salt pork meat. The voice nervously thanked her and disappeared in the night. Josh and Reuben were not allowed to say anything. Papa Eli warned the boys to never say a word about what they saw.

Eli told the boys about the Northern star and watching for moss growing on the north side of the trees down by the creek. Someday, they would understand why the slaves would run away so they would be free. There were several patches of trees that offered refuge and directions to the fleeing slaves.

One morning Eli found a young boy about the age of Reuben hiding among the tobacco leaves. The leaves were so broad that the little fellow could not be seen from a distance. They scared each other. Eli asked him his name and where was he coming from. He said,

22

"My name is Joplin, but they call me 'Jop'. I come from Massa Nash's plantation. I been runnin' three days looking fo' my folks. They was sold last week and I was left behind."

Eli offered him his lunch, which he gladly accepted, and took off running into the thick grove of trees which led to the creek heading North.

About a month later, Eli had another chance to talk briefly to a fugitive slave. It was almost daybreak and Eli was preparing to take one of his trips to pick up supplies for Master Lloyd. This particular morning, as he was busily hooking up the mules to the wagon, a tall, thin, very frightened, runaway slave suddenly stepped out of the barn and begged him not to call for help. He explained,

"I 'scaped from massa Owen's place in Tennessee. I'm on ma way north where I can cross the Ohio River and make it ta' Canada. I have a brother that 'scaped some months back and I'm hopin' to join him soon."

Eli, being a big man, was really not afraid of the slave as much as being caught talking to him. Eli in no way wanted to risk the punishment of having his family sold or separated from the children. Eli asked if he had a name. He said,

"They call me Jobe."

Since it was so early in the morning, there was not much traffic on the main path. Eli asked Jobe to stay in the barn while he filled and spread the straw over the bottom of the wagon. Then Jobe got in and lay very flat while Eli covered him up. Jobe was very grateful and careful not to move. As Eli hooked up the mules and started out, he

23

took a little side trip down by the creek near the thick trees and pretended to let the mules drink while Jobe slid from under the straw. He quickly moved into the water and headed north toward Ohio. Eli's heart was beating so hard he could literally feel it pounding through his raggedy shirt. Eli feared being caught. After he picked up his supplies, he tried to dismiss what had happened, but somehow the young man had made an impression upon him. He sighed deeply and whispered,

"One day, dear Lord, one day."

He gave the mules a 'giddy-up' and headed back to the plantation.

As the hot summer months turned to the cool days of fall, it was time to harvest the fields of dried tobacco, as well as tend to the last of the vegetables left in the garden. Most of the vegetables, turnips, potatoes, and squash were either canned or stored in a cool root cellar under the Master's house. All the fruit was picked from the trees and neatly placed in the cellar before the first signs of winter.

Leah had waited until she was getting bigger and bigger and it was getting harder to conceal that she was pregnant. She finally told Josh and Reuben that she was expecting a baby sometime in November. Miss Sarah already suspected something, but had not openly asked Leah if she was pregnant. Pearlie knew because Leah had confided in her as they walked to work daily. Pearlie assured Leah that she would be there to help her with the delivery of her new baby. Leah took a few minutes from her busy household chores to let Miss Sarah know that she was expecting in the late fall. Miss Sarah showed some compassion toward Leah who was faithful to her and the family. She offered her a few things that her children no longer needed and told her she had clothes and items for the baby. Leah thanked her, being somewhat surprised, at her rare generosity.

As the fall days passed, Leah routinely entered the cabin after a long days work; she always looked forward to relaxing with her sewing and quilting sitting in the old rocking chair. She would wait for Eli and the boys to come home from their chores in the field and finish work around the cabin. The boys were good about bringing in the wood to make the fire. Eli would sometimes help make the meal. Once in a while, Miss Sarah would offer her families' leftovers to Leah. This was always appreciated since Leah was nearing time to deliver. She was frequently exhausted after a days work at the mansion. Her feet were beginning to swell and the walk to and from the log cabin was getting harder each day.

Leah began to sense a change in the weather and realized her time to deliver was drawing near. Pearlie was keeping an eye on Leah and noticed how tired she became at the end of each day. On a cold night when the full moon was bright, Eli went next door and got Pearlie to come stay with Leah. He did not know the first thing to do to help Leah, nor did he know much about birthing babies, only birthing the farm animals. The boys made a big fire in the cooking stove and filled the pots full of water. They sat quietly waiting for Pearlie to tell them what to do. Pearlie prepared her usual herbs and drugs to help with the pain of childbirth. Leah was ready for delivery. Minutes before midnight on November 28, 1854, Leah gave birth to a healthy baby girl. There was great excitement and joy when the baby cried immediately. Josh and Reuben were excited to have a sister. Eli danced and cried as he held the new baby girl in his arms. He raised her to the heavens and gave thanks to God. They decided to name her Delcy, after an aunt who lived in Africa. They knew they would never be able to return to their homeland. Naming her Delcy acknowledged their African heritage as they continued to extend their family in America.

CHAPTER 4—1854-LEAH REMINISCES

After the birth of Delcy, the family provided her with loving attention. Josh and Reuben adored her and Papa Eli spent time helping Leah care for her. Since she was born during the fall, chores around the Master's house were far less demanding than the daily grind of tending crops from sunup to sundown. Eli and the boys stayed busy repairing worn equipment and tending the livestock. Sometimes twice a day they would split wood for both their cabin and the master's house. In the morning they would make certain all the animals were fed and the cows milked. Leah did most of the sewing and quilting during the cold fall and winter days. She especially enjoyed quilting the beautiful patterns shared by Pearlie. Delcy was always by her side well wrapped in quilts to keep her warm.

When Delcy was barely two weeks old, Leah returned to the Master's house and resumed her usual household chores. At least she didn't have to take Delcy out in the cold the first two weeks. Josh and Reuben cut and stacked firewood so the little log cabin was always warm and cozy. Before the cold weather set in, Eli had packed mud into the cracks around the window and door which helped to keep the drafts of the howling winds from entering during the winter.

Delcy was a happy baby. She had facial features similar to Eli. She had big piercing eyes and high cheekbones that set her apart from Leah's features. Leah had a gentle look about her face. She was a very slim and petite woman, weighing a little more than 120 pounds. Eli was over six feet tall and topped the scale at 210 pounds. Reuben was a lot like Eli and Josh resembled Leah. Josh was sensitive to the harsh treatment of Master Lloyd and often cried, unlike Reuben, who was often angry about the treatment of slaves. Even though Josh was small for his age, he had a husky body and was very strong.

Sometimes at night Leah would reflect back to Africa where she longed for the life they had before word spread throughout the villages that Africans were being captured and taken from their homeland. The bearded white men ran through their villages grabbing men, women and children, chaining them together. Those captured were made to walk across the hot earth to several holding cells, then placed on big slave ships. Leah had lived in fear of this day. The European slave catchers were ruthless and cruel. They were paid well to catch as many Africans as a merchant's ship could hold. The captives were chained together while they were prepared for the long, torturous voyage across the Atlantic to America.

When Leah, Eli and the two boys were captured, everyone in the small village was chained together except for the old, sick, and weak. She could not forget the panic and shock during the long walk to the ship. They had never been that far from their village, so everything was very strange and frightening.

As Leah looked at Delcy sleeping quietly in her little box beside the potbellied stove that warmed the cabin, she wondered what Delcy's future would be. Delcy had a disposition that was restless, unlike the boys. Oh, how Leah wished for Africa and freedom for her family. Most of all, she longed for a better life for the children. Josh and Reuben would never have the chance to play with the other boys or follow the men to the wooded areas to collect firewood and bamboo that was used to make baskets and mats. Growing up in Africa as a young man meant leaving early in the morning on hunting trips and returning late in the evening with fresh meat. The whole village shared the kill and celebrated with song and dance. Leah missed the children's laughter and comfort of the older women in the village.

Leah did not have much time to reminisce about her family in Africa. She always intended to tell the boys about life in their native country. Now that Delcy had arrived, Leah made a vow to share as many of the stories with the children as she and Eli could remember. She wanted her children to be able to pass the stories on to their children for generations to come.

Leah looked around the cabin and everyone was asleep. She quietly tucked the children in and sat for a while in the rocker and drifted off to sleep watching Delcy sleep peacefully.

The next morning was routine, except she prepared to take Delcy to work with her. Because the weather was cold, Leah carefully bundled Delcy in warm quilts before placing her in a sling over her shoulders to make the trip to Master Lloyd's house. Leah would have to carry Delcy with her as she did her chores, since there was no convenient place to lay her down in order to keep an eye on her.

Miss Sarah did not make it convenient for Leah to care for Delcy. She even made the remark that Delcy was one more mouth to feed. Leah resented the comment and quickly clutched Delcy closely to her body as a gesture to Miss Sarah that she was more than just another slave. Leah had a way of letting Miss Sarah know that her comment was hurtful. Leah responded by letting Miss Sarah know that Delcy was special to her and her family. She did not have to worry about Leah slacking on her household tasks. Leah was even more careful by attempting to avoid Miss Sarah as she went about doing her job. Leah knew Miss Sarah quite well and knew how hurtful and sharp-tongued she could be. Leah knew the winter months were long and contact was unavoidable. She didn't mind carrying Delcy around. She could nurse her and talk to her whenever she was awake. Delcy slept quietly the first few months, waking only when it was time to nurse and have her diaper changed.

Leah was a good cook. One of her special meals for the Sheff family was boiled turnips, and stewed apples from the cellar and roast pork shoulder from the smoke house. With every meal she served a fresh loaf of bread with sweet churned butter. This was Master Lloyd's favorite, especially the fresh buttermilk from the churn. Once a week all the beds were changed and the mattresses and pillows were fluffed and fresh linen was put on every bed. Strangely, there was one room that Leah never serviced. Most of the children's rooms were on the second floor of the mansion except for the one on the third floor near the attic. Miss Sarah showed Leah the room when she first arrived four years ago but asked her not to service the room.

Washing and ironing became difficult for Leah during the winter months. The fire in the big old stove in the wash house kept the building fairly warm. Once the water was hot, Leah would toss a bar of lye soap made from fat meat into the tub. The soap would begin to melt and make large lathering suds when Leah would scrub the clothes on the old washboard. Every piece of clothing was spotless. Leah would then use the second tub for rinsing. Afterward, she would wring out by hand all the extra water and hang the clothes to dry. Sometimes the clothes would freeze before drying. It was an amusing sight to see Master Lloyd's 'long johns' hanging on the clothesline as stiff as a board. Leah hated the idea of bringing in the frozen clothes and hanging them in the wash- house to dry. After everything dried Leah would start ironing, which would take the greatest part of the day. Everything was ironed. She would make a big fire in the cook stove and set two or three cast irons on the stove to heat at once and begin pressing the sheets and pillowcases. It took more time to press the ruffled petticoats and dresses than it did to iron the men's work and dress clothes. Leah was a beautiful laundress. She hoped someday to teach Delcy how to properly iron clothes. There was money to be made if a free person were asked to do other people's laundry.

CHAPTER 5—ANNA, THE HIDDEN CHILD OF MASTER LLOYD AND MISS SARAH

Anna was born shortly after Pearlie arrived on the Sheff plantation. Pearlie remembered how sick Miss Sarah was during her pregnancy. Master Lloyd gave Pearlie strict orders to never leave Miss Sarah alone. Pearlie had a room next to Miss Sarah so she could care for her night and day. Miss Sarah would always shout orders,

"Pearlie, bring me a cup of tea."

"Pearlie, fix my pillow."

Sometimes Pearlie could not sleep for Miss Sarah calling her all the time. Then, one morning, Miss Sarah went into labor when her water broke. Pearlie began to prepare her special herbs to help ease the pain of birth as she had done many times before. She prepared the bed for giving birth so Miss Sarah would be comfortable.

After a long day of labor, now going into the evening, Miss Sarah had not delivered. Pearlie called for Master Lloyd to get on his horse and ride to Georgetown, a little village about thirty miles away, to get the only doctor in the area. Seemingly, hours had passed before he returned and it was now nearing twelve hours since Miss Sarah's water had broken. A little after noon the next day, Pearlie and old Doc Beckins helped Miss Sarah deliver her second child, a baby girl they named Anna. She was born breech birth with the umbilical cord wrapped around her neck. She was a very sick baby. No one expected her to live.

After a few months, Anna was found to be blind and non-responsive to Pearlie and Miss Sarah. She was unable to hold her head up or move her arms and legs. Pearlie knew there was something very wrong with Anna. After six months, Miss Sarah refused to nurse or care for Anna. The attic room on the third floor was prepared as a nursery. This locked room was where Anna would spend the rest of her life. Pearlie was ordered to keep the door locked, but make certain Anna had what she needed. The tiny baby was underweight and difficult to feed. Miss Sarah rarely visited Anna, therefore, she began to bond with Pearlie. Leah knew never to get into a discussion with Miss Sarah about the child, because this angered her to have to talk about Anna. Leah avoided saying anything to anyone about the hidden child.

CHAPTER 6—1855: WINTER TURNS TO SPRING

As winter gradually turned to spring, Delcy became more active and less willing to stay strapped to Leah. She was gaining weight and getting too heavy for Leah to carry around while she continued to work. Delcy seemed to want attention when her mother was the busiest. All the same, Leah was a very fussy mother and always attempted to address the needs of Delcy as much as possible.

It appeared as though all the chores centered around planting and caring for the crops. As spring turned into summer, most of the farm animals had babies and Josh and Reuben especially enjoyed playing with the small animals.

Delcy was beginning to notice her brothers as they played in the cabin. Josh and Reuben adored her and spent much of their free time playing with her. She laughed out loud and had a big smile that covered her little round face. By the time Delcy was two, she was very independent and curious about many things on the plantation. Josh and Reuben took good care of her when Mama Leah was unable to take her to work. Sometimes Delcy would cry to follow Mama Leah to work. Leah was very careful not to bring Delcy to work with her when special events were planned. When Miss Sarah was having guests, and using her best china and silver, it was not a good idea for a curious baby to be around.

Mama Leah realized that the boys were now young men and it was becoming more difficult to convince them that the plantation would be their life's work. Josh and Reuben were beginning to challenge Eli and Leah about their own freedom. Why did they aid so many fugitive slaves and still live under the rules of Master Lloyd? They saw several run-away slaves a week seeking food and a place to rest overnight. The boys knew the perfect place in the barn behind the stable where the slaves could hide. Often at night they would slip food out to the barn to the young fugitives. Josh and Ruben were becoming less fearful about the consequences for aiding the slaves. Their willingness to take risks was becoming a great concern to their parents. Eli and Leah knew it was a matter of time before their own sons would want to take their freedom into their own hands. On the plantation Eli and Leah sensed a feeling of unrest among the other young slaves.

One morning when Leah and Delcy were preparing to go to Master Lloyd's house to start breakfast, Leah noticed two strangers standing beside their horses talking to Master Lloyd. She felt as though she knew one of the strangers but was not sure. As Leah drew closer to the house, she recognized one of the men as Zac Wallace, the slave broker that had bought them six years ago from the auction steps in Annapolis, Maryland. How could she ever forget that scrubby face and deceitful personality? Her heart began to race with fear. Why would he be visiting Master Lloyd if it were not to sell off the slaves? After all, that was his business: selling and purchasing slaves. All day Leah worked in fear. She could hardly wait to get home to share what she saw with Eli. The first thing that crossed her mind was that Master Lloyd was planning on selling the boys. She had overheard a group of plantation owners talking about the hard times on their plantations because the slaves were escaping in large numbers and there were hardly any dependable ones left to plant and tend the crops.

At other times the men talked about the possibility of a Civil War. They wanted the South to become their own nation, and the North would become independent of the South. Leah was beginning to tie everything together. She worried about the safety of the boys if they were sold to another plantation far away. She feared they would run for freedom and perhaps be caught or killed.

As the year 1860 approached and a new President was campaigning for office, the talk on the plantations was both frightful and hopeful. There was news about a possible war between the states that might eventually set the slaves free. Leah became vigilant and clung onto every word that was spoken at the dinner table. Delcy, now six, was big enough to be helpful, but also curious enough to ask questions about the visitors. Leah tried to keep her busy and away from the Master's house.

Delcy would take water to Papa Eli, Josh, and Reuben as they worked in the fields. Also, she would feed the chickens and ducks in the morning and evening. She would rattle the corn in her little tin bucket and the ducks and chickens would follow her to the feeding trough. She even attempted to milk the cow with one hand. Eli would let her try even though he was not sure she was big enough to handle milking. Sometimes the old cow would kick the bucket over and Eli feared Delcy could get hurt.

During the fall of 1860, there was a feeling of restlessness among the Sheff family and the servants. The fugitive slaves that would cross the plantation were talking about freedom and the war that was brewing in the South over slavery. Master Lloyd began to fear the loss of Josh and Reuben. There was always the possibility of selling them before they had a chance to run. The thought of selling the boys terrified Eli and Leah. Master Lloyd made every effort to keep the news of escaping slaves and the tension between the North and South from the slaves, but to no avail. Leah listened to the visitors talk to Master Lloyd about the economic loss to the plantations if the slaves were set free. Josh, now 15, and Reuben, 17, were aware of the forthcoming war and it was hard to convince them to stay on the plantation. They knew if they left, it would create a hardship for Papa Eli, but the options to stay were not good either. Leah and Eli discussed with the boys the dangers of war and the hopeful desire for their freedom.

The Confederate Army recruiters were already scouring the country in the South, enlisting white soldiers for the war. At the beginning of the war in 1861, it was general knowledge that the white officers and recruits did not trust the slaves to carry weapons. The soldiers feared not only for their lives, but also repercussions and revenge on their families. Retaliation against the masters by the slaves was one of the greatest fears of the South in arming slaves to fight on the side of the Confederates.

Josh and Reuben stayed on the plantation during the winter of 1861, but in the spring of 1862 and the war casualties were mounting on both sides, Josh and Reuben quietly bid Eli, Leah and Delcy goodbye. They headed on horseback toward Ohio, going north to join the Union Army. Under pressure from both black and white antislavery leaders, the first African-American regiment was formed. Josh and Reuben joined the segregated army fighting on the side of the Union. No one ever heard from them again. If they survived the war, they never returned to the Sheff plantation. They possibly went on to freedom in another part of the country, or they died in battle as did so many other blacks. During the war, the labor in the fields rested on the shoulders of Eli, Benjamin and Minnie Paine, two faithful servants who were left behind.

CHAPTER 7—1861-1865: THE CIVIL WAR DAYS

Life on the plantation during the Civil War between 1861 and 1865 was unbearable. There was fear everywhere of Yankee soldiers invading the homes and destroying everything. In most instances, the women and children were the only ones left to keep the plantations going. The few slaves that remained were either too old to leave the plantation or had no place to go. Most of the able bodied slaves had long fled the fields and work places in large numbers. Some of the younger slaves were forced to join the Confederate Army. Many defected north to fight on the side of the Union. There was the promise of freedom if the North defeated the South. As the war progressed, the word of freedom was spreading rapidly throughout the South and North. Slaves were beginning to rebel against the harsh treatment of the slave masters. Many masters tried to prohibit the slaves from escaping but to no avail. Many slaves left the plows in the fields and ran for freedom. There was not enough money in the South to finance the war. With few slaves to tend the crops, the war was using up a large portion of the economic gains generated from the sale of crops. The South was slowly becoming economically devastated. The free labor of slavery was rapidly dwindling and no one was sure when it would all end.

The year 1863 at the height of the Civil War, Josh and Reuben had not made contact with their family. Delcy had just turned nine and the workload on the Sheff plantation was more demanding of her, Eli, and Leah. The household and field work were endless for Eli who worked from sunup until sundown. The job of hauling water, splitting the wood, and caring for the work animals was left for Eli, Leah, and Delcy. Because of the advancing age of their neighbors, Benjamin and Minnie Paine, they were only capable of sharing some of the less strenuous farm activities such as caring for the pigs and chickens, collecting eggs, and doing various other odd jobs as required by Master Lloyd and Miss Sarah.

Master Lloyd had cut the tobacco crop by half since he no longer had the help or the resources to harvest the usual acreage. Pearlie continued to work in the master's house. Most of her time was spent taking care of Anna since the other Sheff children were gone from the plantation. Miss Sarah rarely said much about how long Pearlie took to do her work.

Both Master Lloyd and Miss Sarah were concerned about the accumulated debt that they had from borrowing money against the plantation in order to meet the farming expenses. Help was short and they could not count on free slave labor anymore. Slaves enroute to the North frequently passed the Sheff plantation seeking food, shelter, and medicine. Most would hide out in the corncrib or tobacco barn, seeking a few hours of rest and sleep before continuing their journey north. Eli and Leah remained cautious in offering help to the fleeing slaves. Delcy was willing to risk the harsh punishment from Master Lloyd if he caught her helping the slaves. Delcy would slip the fleeing slaves food and clothing. One day she was caught taking clothes off the clothes line to give to a fleeing family. Master Lloyd was so angry with Delcy that he gave her a severe whipping. She was so strong willed that Leah and Eli knew that the life ahead for Delcy would be a difficult one without their care and guidance.

Delcy was very unhappy on the plantation. Seemingly, she could do nothing right, at least not to satisfy Master Lloyd. She was very bitter and resented the day-to-day struggle imposed on her family. At times, the struggle to keep the crops cultivated and the garden and animals tended seemed endless. The lack of help was a problem on nearly every plantation. One day Master Lloyd made a deal with another plantation master to hire out Eli for a day. Eli was very hesitant in going to some one else's plantation to work. He had done that once before and found the workload was so hard that he was sick for several days afterward from heat exhaustion. Delcy could see the stress taking its toll on her father. He was the type of person who rarely complained to the master. Because he was somewhat slow in making the journey, Delcy spoke abruptly and sarcastically to Master Lloyd in defense of Eli. Master Lloyd slapped Delcy so hard she spun around and hit the ground. Eli became so angry he picked up Delcy and walked toward the cabin as though the day was over. Master Lloyd did not pursue Eli. For the first time Eli truly felt like running away and taking his family. Perhaps Master Lloyd thought the same thing, because he never approached Eli again about working for another master.

After the experience with Delcy, Eli hoped there would be some changes for the better. The old plantation was gradually falling into disarray as the war continued. The crops were less profitable and extra help was no longer available. There was no money to buy lumber to fix fences or repair the house. The old cooking stove had seen better days and the few animals left would graze the pastures that were becoming stripped of their hay and barley. Eli and Leah were weary and unable to keep up with the demands on them. Each did the best they could to prepare the meals and tend to the farming chores.

As Delcy became even more rebellious and sassy to Master Lloyd, her treatment became more harsh and severe. Tensions mounted between Master Lloyd and Eli and Leah over the treatment of Delcy. One morning when everyone arose for the task assignments for the day, Delcy was gone. She had slipped out of the cabin during the night. Her parents' fear was intense because they worried about how a young slave girl could survive the wilderness, and if she could by chance meet someone traveling the Underground Railroad. Before daybreak, Delcy returned, exhausted. She had been unable to continue the escape because she had never been off the plantation in her life, so she was unfamiliar with the surroundings. Leah and Eli were extremely happy to see her and glad that she had returned safely. Fortunately, Master Lloyd never learned of her attempt to escape.

One year later, 1864, the Civil War, in its third year, continued to drag on. The Sheff plantation was falling deeper and deeper in debt. Theirs was not the only plantation the local banks had foreclosed on. The plantations were in debt for seed, supplies, and parts to repair equipment. Still unable to purchase seed for spring planting and to repair the worn out equipment, Master Lloyd made one more plea to the bank for an extension on his loan but to no avail. Master Lloyd had one option: that was to sell Eli and Leah so he could at least buy food and needed household items to support the family. Word of selling Eli and Leah outraged Delcy to the extent that her thoughts of retaliation intensified against Master Lloyd. After fourteen long toiling and faithful years of sweat and tears, Eli and Leah would be sold. The Sheff's decided Delcy would remain on the plantation because she was young, strong and healthy and could be useful in the house and in the fields. Despite her many good qualities, Delcy was known for her fiery temper. The Sheff's tolerated Delcy's outbursts because she was was a valuable asset to their plantation.

One Monday morning when Leah and Delcy were on their way to the Master's house to do the washing as they did every Monday morning, they saw from a distance Master Lloyd talking to Zac Wallace. He always brought bad news. Leah and Delcy became afraid. Everyone knew that Master Lloyd was so broke that he didn't know where his next piece of bread was coming from. Master Lloyd waited until Eli came to the house to fill the wash tubs with water and help build the fire under the big tubs as he usually did, since Josh and Reuben were gone. While standing near the laundry tubs, Master Lloyd broke the news to Eli and Leah that he would have to sell them because he needed the money. Delcy, now ten, was devastated. Miss Sarah showed great remorse at the selling of Leah. At least the sale was private and they did not have to stand on an auction step as they had fourteen years ago when Zac purchased them for Master Lloyd. Eli was a faithful and good worker. He always did as he was told. Eli and Leah sobbed as they clung to each other.

Zac borrowed a wagon from Master Lloyd so Eli and Leah could pack a few personal things that they wanted to take. There was not much from which to choose. Most of the household items were in poor condition, like everything else on the plantation. Leah decided to leave the rocking chair and other items for Delcy since she would remain there under the supervision of Pearlie. As the wagon pulled up in front of the cabin Leah and Eli hugged Delcy with all their strength and vowed to see each other again. Delcy cried uncontrollably. She believed her parents were going a long way. Zac tied his horse to the back of the wagon and once again chained Eli and Leah to the wagon and climbed into the seat, gave the mules a crack and the long journey to the Jenkins plantation in Tennessee became a reality.

Master Jenkins had offered Master Lloyd a good price for the two. He had a smaller tobacco plantation and the workload would not be as heavy for Eli and Leah.

As the wagon pulled onto the dusty road leading from the plantation, Delcy ran behind the wagon until she was too tired to keep up, then she fell to the ground sobbing as she watched the wagon carrying Mama Leah and Papa Eli disappear into the dust. As she pulled herself off the ground and slowly walked toward the empty cabin that sat on the edge of the tobacco field, Pearlie was there to comfort her. She explained that Master Lloyd was facing hard times, and it was hard to let them go. This made no sense to Delcy. She asked Pearlie,

"Why didn't they sell us as a family? Why was I left alone?"

44

Pearlie had seen families sold and separated many times before but she did not have answers for Delcy. As she pulled away from Pearlie and entered the empty cabin she stared at the rocking chair that had the same old straw stuffed cushion that Mama Leah had made many years ago. She remembered how the old rocker had been used to rock her when she was small and how Mama Leah would mend and quilt way into the night sitting by the lamplight. Delcy sat gently in the old rocker and began to sing the song Leah had sung to her when she was a baby.

"Sweet little baby girl, born in the cold of night, nobody knows about you. Sweet little baby girl, so quiet as you sleep, nobody knows what lies ahead, so sleep, gently, sleep." Delcy wept for hours and finally fell asleep in the wee hours of the morning.

Delcy was certainly in no mood to walk to Master Lloyd's house. After all, she had rarely made the trip alone. Mama Leah had always been beside her. That was their time to laugh and talk. This day was different from any other day in her life. Pearlie made her way to the house without Delcy. Delcy thought about running away again and working in the war camps that she had heard about but she didn't know her way. She had mixed feelings about how to get even with Master Lloyd for selling Mama and Papa.

CHAPTER 8—1865: DELCY ALONE

Delcy returned to the Master's house several days later. Miss Sarah showed no compassion toward Delcy and displayed her usual abrupt and curt disposition. Delcy had become accustomed to her behavior. But she could not help thinking about the law that was signed by President Lincoln declaring that slavery no longer existed, and that all slaves were to be set free.

"What kind of freedom were the slaves promised?"

Delcy certainly did not see much freedom on the plantation. Master Lloyd ignored the Proclamation setting slaves free. He tried to say that slavery was good.

He even talked about how good he had been to Leah and Eli.

"It only made me mad to know that he thought I would fall for something like that," Delcy told Pearlie.

Delcy began to listen carefully to the conversations and questions that Master Lloyd would be discussing with other plantation owners. She heard all about the war and how the slaves continued to fight to set themselves free. She really wanted to hear more about freedom. Mama Leah and Papa Eli had always promised her that someday she would be free.

As the months passed, Pearlie was always there for Delcy when she felt lonely or when there was tension building between her and Master Lloyd. Pearlie could sense that Delcy was bitter and angry a great deal of the time. She often broke things or omitted doing a certain task that was required of the house help, and when she was corrected, she displayed a hostile disposition that often got her into a great deal of trouble. One time Master Lloyd requested a fresh glass of buttermilk from the cellar. When Delcy brought him the milk it was spoiled. After questioning Delcy, he discovered that she had left the top off the buttermilk and the flies had spoiled the milk. To punish her, he made her drink the spoiled milk. Delcy became very sick. She vomited for hours, after which he proceeded to beat her with a buggy whip until large welts appeared all over her back and shoulders. Delcy was treated and comforted by Pearlie. After that whipping, Delcy made a vow that Master Lloyd would never beat her again. She often plotted his death in the most severe way and wished the most awful things would happen to him. Her thoughts were filled with ways to destroy Master Lloyd for all the hurt and pain he had brought upon her and her family.

In the year 1865, a year after the sale of Eli and Leah, the Civil war ended. There was even more talk about the slaves being free, especially in the North. Many free blacks chose not to return to the harsh southern plantation life. Those that did return found working conditions had not changed much. Most plantations were in ruin and the crops that once flourished at the hands of slave labor were gone. Delcy noticed freed blacks crossing the tobacco plantation headed north to find their families or to find a better life. Some free blacks and their families began the move westward where jobs or land were, they hoped, more available. All Delcy could think of was how trapped she felt on Master Lloyd's plantation with no place to go. As she settled back into her routine of cleaning and helping with the farm chores, she heard talk of really bad things happening to free blacks who tried to leave the South. She did not have a clear idea of everything that was said as she eaves-dropped on the dinner conversation between Miss Sarah and Master Lloyd. Certainly she did not want to be caught by any roaming white vigilante group looking to do harm to runaway free blacks. Her fears forced her to remain on the Sheff plantation.

As Delcy was fast approaching her fifteenth birthday, she began reflecting often about the family that she once loved and counted on to always be there for her. She thought that everything good was gone. She missed Mama Leah and Papa Eli. She wondered if they were free, and if they would they keep their promise to come back to get her. At every opportunity, Delcy displayed a rebellious attitude toward Master Lloyd. One afternoon during supper, Delcy spilled a pot of hot tea that landed on Master Lloyd. Before she could move and clean up the spill, Master Lloyd beat and abused her. Seemingly, all his anger for the many things he once tolerated from her was now directed toward her behavior and attitude toward him. Delcy tried to defend herself against Master Lloyd by abruptly leaving the house. She was frightened, for she had never physically stood up to Master Lloyd. This time somehow seemed different.

"If I am free, why do I feel more like a slave than ever before?"

Delcy ran all the way to the cabin and rocked nervously while trying to find comfort. Master Lloyd had been angry with her before, but never like this. Pearlie helped clean up the supper dishes and hurriedly made her way down the dusty path to see about Delcy.

Pearlie tried to comfort her by hugging her and wiping away her tears. Pearlie understood the harshness of plantation life as she spoke gently to Delcy about her own life as a young girl and how to avoid the wrath of Master Lloyd. Delcy didn't see any way out. After several hours of talking to Pearlie, Delcy prepared for bed and Pearlie went to her little cabin next door.

During the night, Delcy was awakened by a rattle at the door. She was terrified. She could not imagine who it was. Before she could sit up in bed, Master Lloyd broke down the cabin door. She tried to fight him off, but he ripped off her clothes. He raped her although she continued to struggle to free herself. Master Lloyd shouted at her, trying to humiliate her, so she would feel less than the strong human being she grew to be. In his perverted way, he was trying to "teach her" that she was nothing without him and what he could provide for her.

The brutal attack left Delcy distraught and afraid. Pearlie came over to check on Delcy and found her huddled in the corner of the room with her face buried in her hands, clothes ripped off, and the cabin in disarray. Delcy tried to pull herself together to explain to Pearlie what had happened to her in the middle of the night. Pearlie comforted Delcy and tended to the wounds and bruises left on her body and face as a result of the assault.

Delcy became extremely depressed and found it difficult to get up in the morning and go to the Sheff house. She tried to avoid Master Lloyd by working outside and tending to the animals and garden. Because the Sheff's could not afford to hire more help, it became an almost impossible task for Pearlie to keep up the household and care for Anna. After the small garden was harvested, and the work outside diminished, Delcy returned inside to the Master's house, carefully avoiding Master Lloyd.

Several months after the sexual assault, Delcy realized that she was expecting a child. The fear of being pregnant overwhelmed her. Miss Sarah asked prying questions of her. They were all directed toward her gaining weight and the noticeable change in the clothes that Delcy chose to wear in order to conceal her pregnancy. Delcy often chose to ignore the questions and quickly proceeded to prepare the meals and do required housework. The more noticeable Delcy's pregnancy became, the more curious Miss Sarah became. Also, Delcy became more withdrawn and depressed. Miss Sarah knew Delcy was pregnant. She even implied that Delcy had been with someone that stopped by the plantation looking for work.

As fall set in on the plantation, Delcy collected small scraps of fabric and other used pieces of linen and old clothes given to her by Miss Sarah to prepare for the baby. The first thing she made was a small patch quilt that had many old familiar pieces left behind by Mama Leah and Papa Eli. Pearlie was cautious when talking to Delcy about the baby. She knew how sensitive and depressed Delcy would become. However, Delcy knew that Pearlie would be there for her. Delcy continued to be cautious around Master Lloyd. She was afraid he might decide to beat her and cause her to lose the baby. Therefore, she tried to avoid any confrontations of any kind with him. All Delcy could think of at this point, was the life she wanted for her child, and just how protective she would have to be. As winter approached, her pregnancy was more obvious and she became even more withdrawn. Master Lloyd was very nervous around Delcy and at one point commented,

"I didn't mean you no harm, I just wanted to teach you a lesson."

Delcy turned sixteen in November. She had made a few small gowns and prepared a box that she kept under the bed with fresh scraps of white linen. As the winter snow began to fall and the Christmas season was nearing, Miss Sarah decorated the Sheff home. In the meantime, Delcy became increasingly tired and less able to do what was required of her. As Christmas Eve approached, Delcy felt differently and knew her time was near.

Late Christmas Eve, after fixing dinner for the Sheff family, Delcy went into labor. She hurriedly finished her work and headed home. She reached the cabin before dark. She filled the wooden bin with fire logs and all the extra pots and pans with snow and ice before resting for a minute. Delcy knew Pearlie was home because she could see her footprints in the snow leading to her door. She was trying to decide when to call Pearlie. She knew she moved around much slower now and it would take her a little more time to get through the snow to reach the cabin. Delcy was tired and decided to wait a while before knocking on Pearlie's door. Wearily, she sat quietly in the rocker and reminisced about how things used to be.

CHAPTER 9—1870: DELCY GIVES BIRTH TO LIZZIE

Christmas Eve 1870 was one of the most chilling days of winter. The wind sliced through the cracks of the cabin. Snow had been falling all day and now it was knee high between the cabin and the woodpile, which was at least fifty feet from the front door. The old cabin was one of three still standing on the Sheff's tobacco plantation in Leesburg, Kentucky.

As Delcy sat alone in the cabin, her mind wandered. "Where did the time go?" she thought. "The days of laughter from the slave children playing in the late evenings after tending to the master's farm chores, all gone. The bright green burly tobacco leaves glistening from the morning dew, just about all gone. Only a few acres here lately to tend." She remembered how they used to stand on the edge of the fields where the cabins were, straining their eyes to see as far as they could see. It seemed as though they could look for miles and see the beautiful pink blossoms that draped the top of each stalk of tobacco as harvest time drew near. The rows between the plants were so straight they could see each little leaf that grew on the tobacco stalk.

Behind the cabins on their walk to the Master's house, they would pass the barnyard. The farm animals were well cared for because Delcy and her family made sure they always had plenty of food and water. Sometimes, she thought, the animals often fared better than the people did. The chore of feeding the animals was mostly the job of the children. Now the children were all gone. "All grown, I suppose," she sighed out loud. "Don't know why no one would bother coming back here visiting. Most don't care if you are alive or dead. The few cows left in the barnyard give just enough milk for Master Lloyd and the few of us still living in the log cabins. Only three free blacks left. Pearlie next door is the friendliest. She is beginning to have health problems. She must be past forty." Delcy noticed Pearlie prayed a lot as well as talked a lot about life as it used to be. She supposed Pearlie knew more about that than anybody else on the plantation. She had been around, it seemed, forever. She was the one who was birthing babies; people and animals. Pearlie was faithful to Anna. She sighed, "Poor thing, never gets out of that room."

Delcy thought about the times she had to feed the farm animals. Everywhere she looked, there were chickens and ducks. Red ones, speckled ones, white ones with rosy red head cones. They were always pecking and walking in the clean water. Master Lloyd was always yelling to change the water. Those nasty ducks were always making a mess. Every fall they would help kill the older fat ducks. "We would pluck their feathers, especially the soft fuzzy down feathers. We used them to stuff the pillows and bed mattresses for the Master's house. We were thankful to get fresh straw and hay once a year to fill our own home made pillows and bed mats." Now, there were only a few animals left. Most of the animals, except for the two teams of mules, were all gone. "Just like the men folks that kept the plantation going, all gone. Master Lloyd and Miss Sarah don't have any more money. All they talk about is how it used to be. The tobacco crops get smaller and smaller because nobody is around to plant and chop the weeds." Delcy remembered having barely enough food to keep them going. "Times ain't getting any better. Ain't got no help," Delcy huffed out loud. "Master Lloyd and Miss Sarah are treating us like we ain't free." Delcy would see free folks crossing the fields all the time on their way up north looking for their families and work along the way. She couldn't help wondering about what it was truly like to be free.

As Delcy shivered from the cold, she looked around the cabin. It had barely enough furnishings. Against the wall facing east was a wooden bed with a big thick mattress stuffed with fresh straw. It looked lumpy because of a big scrap quilt made from old clothes that covered the bed from side to side. Under the bed was a wooden storage box that held extra clothing, bedding material and scraps of cloth used for mending and quilting. Delcy's mama, Leah, had a gift for sewing and quilting that kept the family with clothes and bedding.

In the middle of the floor was a big wooden table that nearly filled the entire room. Hanging from the ceiling on a big rusty nail was an old kerosene lamp that would sway when the wind whistled. Mama's handmade curtains covered the only window in the cabin. There were two Bentwood chairs at the table and two straight back chairs, hand made by Papa Eli, that were placed near the potbellied stove that was used for cooking and heating the cabin. In one corner the rocking chair made from pecan wood had a well-used woven bottom that looked like a wooden basket made from hand stripped hickory tree bark. The rocker used to belong to Master Lloyd and Miss Sarah, just like most of the furniture.

She remembered watching Mama Leah heat the old iron on the top of the stove. Delcy learned how to press each little scrap of material before neatly shaping it into a little patch for the quilt. Delcy was very handy around the house. Not only was she good at making quilts, but she was also a very good cook. Leah had taught her how to cook, iron, and sew. She thought about how the women would often mend clothes and swap stories and quilt pieces. During the days of plenty, the women would sit around the fire and invent new recipes for fixing the small rations of salt pork, smoked fish, and cornmeal that were issued weekly by the Master. Once in a while, leftover garden vegetables, milk, and cheese were shared for Sunday dinner. Sometimes on Sunday, the other slave families would put all their food rations together and boil up a big supper feast. Everyone would sing and dance. The children especially liked to celebrate birthdays. Little did they know the hardships that lay ahead of them.

As her baby moved inside, she felt warm and sick at the same time. She gently rubbed her tight belly. "This is not the time to be alone" she thought, as she began to tremble with fear at the thought of giving birth. As she rocked from side to side, the birth pains began to come closer and closer. The unborn baby seemed to sense her mother's fear of being alone. Delcy had been alone a lot lately—five years to be exact. Except for Pearlie, life was very sad and dreary. Delcy would have left the Sheff's plantation by now but she knew absolutely no one beyond the fields. What would she do? Where would she go? She felt trapped. She was trapped.

In the silence of the cold night, Delcy could sometimes hear the crackle from the potbellied stove where the fire was beginning to burn out. Sitting in the old rocking chair, the sixteen-year old, ex-slave girl was quickly approaching her time to deliver her first child.

Delcy suddenly felt a sharp pain in her back. She cried as a wave of pain gradually moved through her body. She thought about the presence of Mama Leah and how wise she'd always been in providing words of comfort and advice in difficult times. This had to be the worst Christmas Eve ever. In the past, Christmas had been a merry time for the Brent family. Once again, Delcy reflected on old times. Mama Leah would always make sure that Christmas was special. Delcy remembered Mama Leah making her a doll out of corn shucks and dressing it in a tiny print bandanna and skirt. "I carried it everywhere. I remember how, one day, I left it at old Master Lloyd's house and the next day it was gone. Miss Sarah made like she never saw it, but I knew she was lying. She was so mean; she probably burned it up. I never trusted her anyhow. I cried for hours over my doll. Mama Leah knew how sad I was. One day when my two brothers, Josh and Reuben, finished shucking the corn in the crib for the cattle and the chickens and ducks, they brought home a big hand full of corn shucks. Mama Leah spent nearly all evening making me another doll. After that, she reminded me to always leave my doll at home because Miss Sarah did not love the doll as much as I did. From that time on I never forgot what Mama said about love."

Delcy felt her breathing get harder and she began to sweat. With all the strength she could muster, she made her way through the knee-high snow to the cabin next door where Pearlie lived. Even though Pearlie had no children of her own, she had delivered more babies than she could count on her hands and toes.

Frantically, Delcy called,

"Miss Pearlie, you in there? Miss Pearlie, my baby is coming!"

Miss Pearlie answered Delcy with a calm tone in her voice,

"Delcy, can you make it back to the cabin?"

"Yes," said Delcy.

"The fire is getting low and I am afraid the water got cold."

Pearlie assured Delcy that she would be there as soon as she dressed and put some things in her birthin' bag. She also told Delcy to put another log in the stove and put the ice and snow on the stove to melt before she got there.

As Delcy made her way back to the cabin she tried to remember what she had seen Mama Leah do in times like these. She did what Pearlie told her to do. She removed the neatly folded clean linen from the large wooden box under the bed and placed it on the straight back chair by the stove. She had previously filled the small wooden box from the barn with fresh straw to use as a cradle.

Time was moving quickly. Delcy sat in the rocker and rocked impatiently. She cradled her arms around her belly wondering what was keeping Miss Pearlie from coming through the door. She glanced at the old clock ticking on the wall; it was a little past midnight. It was Christmas.

Suddenly, without knocking, Pearlie rushed through the door with a large bag full of prepared homemade remedies. Pearlie had learned from her mother and grandmother which herbs and roots to use and how to mix them to help a woman through birthing. She always wore a neatly pressed white apron and a long gray dress that swept the floor. She hustled around the tiny cabin making preparations for the delivery. Excitingly, Delcy gave out a loud cry. She felt her baby move closer and closer to the birthing position. As Delcy lay in the birthing position, she knew it would not be long before she needed to push. Delcy began to feel the pain of childbirth. Pearlie held her hand and Delcy squeezed with all her strength. With one big push, Delcy delivered her child.

Pearlie carefully washed the baby with warm water, wrapped her in the linen and the little quilt, and placed her in Delcy's arms. The patch quilt that Delcy had made from scraps of material was just the right size. Pearlie leaned close to Delcy and spoke softly wishing her,

"Merry Christmas. You have been given the greatest gift on this special day."

Delcy asked Pearlie to name the baby girl. She thought this would be the greatest gift for Pearlie. She had never been asked to name a baby. She thought long and hard and decided on Lizzie. This name really pleased Delcy. As she rested with Lizzie snuggled warmly in her arms, she sang softly to her,

"Sweet Little baby girl, beautiful in my sight; nobody knows your name, like the Holy One born on this Night. Sweet little baby girl, so quiet and as you sleep; no one knows what lies ahead, so sleep gently, sleep."

Delcy lay exhausted. It wasn't long before she drifted off to sleep. The long darkness of the night gradually turned to day. The snow finally ended and the sky cleared. The sun's rays on the snow caused it to sparkle like diamonds. When Delcy awoke, she noticed Pearlie moving about quietly adding wood to the fire that had burned low during the night. She had fixed breakfast for Delcy and made sure Lizzie was snug and warm. As Pearlie opened the door, snow fell inside. She quickly swept away the snow in order to make a path to the woodpile. She would not go home until she was sure that Delcy and Lizzie would be okay.

Delcy began to stir around in the room, fussing over Lizzie and making sure the cold weather would not take her child. She knew that many babies died due to the cold and she was not about to let that happen to Lizzie. She tucked her warmly in her little box and moved it closer to the potbellied stove. After Pearlie fed Delcy, she left to prepare the Christmas meal for Master Lloyd and Miss Sarah's family.

Delcy stared into the fire and her thoughts brought her back to when Mama Leah would fix Christmas dinner for the family. It wasn't like the Sheff's but it was a blessing. The slaves that worked in the house had to work on Christmas Day due to all the company the Sheff's would have. The visitors would pull up to the big house in their fancy buggies with the women clothed in their finest dresses and the men in their best suits and hats. They would bring gifts and food sometimes. After the white folks were fed and started dancing and singing, the slaves were allowed to go back to their cabins. The leftovers were always plentiful and divided among those helping in the kitchen. When Mama Leah cooked the leftovers, she would take the hog parts and make the best hog headcheese and sausage. She boiled the feet, ears, and tail and made a pig stew. She added potatoes, turnips, and onions from the cellar. Mama Leah shared her holiday secrets of food preparation with Delcy, who would one day teach Lizzie these traditional recipes.

CHAPTER 10—1871: DELCY GETS MARRIED

Lizzie, born out of violence, was comforted and protected by Delcy. As Delcy told Pearlie the story of how Master Lloyd had raped her, Pearlie listened with compassion. Afterward, Delcy wept bitterly. She wanted so much more for Lizzie than the harshness of life on the Sheff tobacco plantation. Somehow life on the plantation didn't seem much different for the few sharecroppers that now worked the tobacco fields. Even though the slaves were free, Delcy felt trapped on the farm. She often became controlled by fear of violent retaliation against her.

When Lizzie's birth was recorded in the old 1876 family Bible, it read "Born December 25, 1870, Lizzie Brent Sheff." This was Delcy's chance to document history in a way that Lloyd Sheff would never forget the violent act of rape that resulted in the birth of beloved Lizzie.

Delcy soon turned her attention to Lizzie, gently cradling her in her arms as she began to move back and forth in the rocking chair, softly humming the tune she remembered from her mother. Delcy sang the little tune over and over as she nestled her to her breast,

"Sweet baby girl born on Christmas day, no one knows about you. Sweet little baby girl, born to bring joy and peace on this day. Sleep baby Lizzie on this special day."

As time passed and the harsh winter of 1870 gradually turned to spring of 1871, Lizzie was growing healthy and strong. She seemed to have a significant place in Miss Sarah's life as a special child, since she bore some resemblance to Master Lloyd. Miss Sarah had no doubt that Lizzie was a mulatto child fathered by Master Lloyd. However, she never discussed it with Delcy or Master Lloyd. This delicate circumstance was quite common on most plantations in the south.

As Miss Sarah aged, she had not changed much in demeanor; she was still outspoken and demanding. As she grew more feeble from a stroke that left her partially paralyzed on the left side, she continued to give commands for service. All the plantation children were gone and the Sheff children rarely returned to the plantation except for Christmas.

Now that Pearlie was unable to spend much time with Anna, Delcy had to help both Miss Sarah and Anna. Miss Sarah was now frequently left alone; just like Anna locked in the attic room. The Sheff grandchildren rarely saw Miss Sarah and Master Lloyd. Sometimes Miss Sarah talked about missing the children, but then she dismissed the thought and prepared to sit in a big overstuffed chair looking out the dining room window thinking of what used to be. Most of the beauty of the plantation, which included white fences and beautifully maintained flowers and trees, was all gone. Now the fences needed fixing and the flower gardens were all full of weeds.

As the time for spring planting of the tobacco grew near, Master Lloyd found himself in a predicament: a crop to be planted and no help. In order to plant the tobacco before the spring rain, he would need a new sharecropper. After the war, it was common for free blacks to leave the south headed north looking for work. They often wandered from one plantation to another inquiring about sharecropping or other odd jobs.

Over the past few weeks, several ex-slaves had stopped at the Sheff plantation and inquired about work. After a few days they moved on. Master Lloyd was getting older and unable to manage the tobacco planting. He thought about asking the neighboring farmer about sharing field hands, but the neighbor had no one to share. As he leaned on the hitching post in front of the mansion, he thought about the abundance of help and wealth he had access to in the "good old days." He looked around at all the work that needed to be done. He squinted his eyes as he strained to identify the figure walking down the old dusty road leading to the plantation. As the figure drew closer, he moved from the hitching post to greet the man approaching.

The time could not have been better for Neut Smith, a tall ex-slave from Georgia, very robust in stature, looking for work. Master Lloyd offered Neut the opportunity to sharecrop the tobacco, and in return, he would receive a portion of money when the crop was sold.

Delcy could see Neut from the window. She hoped with all her heart that Master Lloyd had hired him. She watched as Master Lloyd showed Neut his living quarters, and then walked him to the fields where the crops would be planted. Neut seemed pleased to have a job and was very polite in accepting the working conditions set forth by Master Lloyd.

Delcy felt that Neut was someone special when she first saw him. She made a point of introducing herself to Neut as she prepared supper for him in the Sheff's kitchen. Neut was very hungry after traveling for days looking for work. Most of his time was spent on the move, walking for miles and eating whenever an act of kindness was shown to him by free blacks. He was pleased to finally get a good hot cooked meal.

Delcy observed that Neut was very kind and gentle. She made small talk with him as she watched him eat. He talked about the cotton plantation in Georgia where he worked as a slave and how he did not want to return to Georgia. Delcy told him about her life as a slave girl on the tobacco plantation and baby Lizzie, who was barely four months old. She wanted someone to share her desire for freedom. She saw in Neut, her chance to leave the plantation so they would have a better life. As Neut finished his dinner, Master Lloyd came to the kitchen and reminded Neut that the breakfast bell rang at six o'clock and he was expected to be ready for work. Neut had much to learn about tobacco. He had always worked in the cotton fields. To him there appeared not to be much difference; he understood that all farming required planting, plowing and harvesting.

As Delcy continued her chores for Miss Sarah, she looked forward to preparing supper for Neut. Supper time was their chance to get to know each other and talk about old times. Neut and Delcy began to establish a special friendship that had prospects of growing into a promising future.

Delcy had never had anyone treat her as kindly as Neut. He was different; he seemed to know how to treat a lady.

Neut Smith had spent the early years of his life on the Murphy plantation working the cotton fields as a boy and later as a blacksmith.

He worked in the stables in the evening caring for the horses after picking cotton all day. At the age of sixteen he began to help the blacksmith shoe the horses as well as repair the harnesses. After the war ended in 1865, Neut had no desire to stay on the Murphy plantation. He worked at a number of odd jobs for the first few years after the war before stopping at the Sheff plantation looking for work. Neut was a man of few words. Although he could recognize some words and math numbers, he could not read and write. He was hard working and honest. If he gave a person his word that something would be done, one could count on it being done.

After a six-month courtship, Neut asked Delcy to marry him. He hoped that he had proved to her that he could be trusted, and promised to love and care for both her and Lizzie as though Lizzie were his own.

Soon after Delcy turned eighteen, Neut and Delcy were married. Delcy got all dressed up in her very best cotton dress. Master Lloyd was relieved because he felt that Delcy wound remain on the plantation if Neut stayed. He knew if she left, he would have no one to care for Sarah and Anna. Little did Lloyd Sheff know the thoughts of leaving the plantation were more frequent.

When Lizzie was two, Delcy gave birth to her second child, a baby boy, on March 4, 1872. They named him Charley. Lizzie was so excited to have a baby brother and was eager to help Mama Delcy care for him.

Neut and Delcy continued to work as sharecroppers on the Sheff plantation. As sharecroppers, they were given a minimal salary at the

65

end of each tobacco season for their work. As Charlie and Lizzie bonded as brother and sister, Lizzie began to assume more and more responsibility. She helped with the farm animals by feeding the chickens and ducks, churning the milk to make butter, and carrying water to the field for Neut and the other workers that would move from farm to farm often working a different plantation every two or three days. There were a large number of day workers because farm work was seasonal. In these lean economic times, most plantation owners could not afford to hire more than one or two full time sharecroppers.

In the spring of 1875, Pearlie became sick and no longer was able to work. Delcy would look in on her daily and make sure she had her meals and fresh water. Delcy and Neut, with two active children, spent as much time as possible with Lizzie and Charlie. Lizzie was a smart little girl. She wanted to learn to read and write like Master Lloyd and Miss Sarah's grandchildren. She became friends with Lucy Bell, Master Lloyd's oldest granddaughter. Lucy Bell would pretend to play school and Lizzie would be her student. Lizzie soon learned to read, write and do simple math problems.

In the fall of 1875, Delcy and Neut had another baby, but it did not live very long. Delcy and her family were all grief stricken when the baby died. In 1877, when Lizzie was seven, Delcy gave birth to their third child, a girl whom they named Mary. Once again, Lizzie helped with the new baby along with her barnyard and household chores. It seemed that with each baby, Lizzie had more and more responsibility.

Mary was a fussy baby and Delcy often had to spend more time nursing and caring for her. It was becoming increasingly difficult to take care of two households. Both Miss Sarah and Pearlie were failing in health and having problems with mobility. Delcy continued to care for Anna and Miss Sarah, but the farm chores were the duty of Neut and the children. Taking the children to work with her, Delcy did all the washing, cooking and cleaning. Charlie followed Lizzie around as she helped with the laundry, hanging clothes on the line to dry, and filling the water tubs. She also carried small pieces of wood and dried corncobs to keep the fire going.

Delcy took good care of Pearlie, as her health continued to decline. In the fall of 1877, Pearlie died at the age of 51. She was buried in the graveyard for slaves on the Sheff plantation. Delcy and her family felt the loss of a dear and devoted friend.

Lizzie was beginning to learn how to quilt, knit, crochet, and cook by watching Mama Delcy. Neut remained in the field for long hours. His time with the family was mainly spent doing chores. After helping Master Lloyd, who was aging, and Miss Sarah who was chronically complaining, Neut managed to provide for the needs of both households. He always split and stacked the wood and kept the water barrels and buckets filled with fresh water from the well.

As months turned to years, 1879 found Delcy, Neut, and the children getting older with seemingly little hope of leaving the Sheff plantation. Lizzie, now nine, remained small for her age while Charlie seven was large for his age. Mary, now two, was relatively happy and required little additional care from Lizzie or Charlie.

During the summer of 1879, Lizzie assumed much more of the plantation duties. When the animals would see her coming with her little buckets of grain and water, they followed her until she fed and watered them. Lizzie was often tired from helping Miss Sarah and the children.

One day Lizzie noticed Mama Delcy was expecting another baby. She did not show her pregnancy until almost time to deliver because she wore large over-the-shoulder aprons that hid her figure. Delcy gave birth to her fourth child on November 18, 1879. It was a baby girl that she named Martha.

Delcy felt the hard times of often not having enough food to feed everybody. Most of the clothes her children wore were handed down from the Sheff grandchildren and patched in many places. Lizzie hardly remembered what it was like to have a new dress made out of flour sacks by Mama Delcy.

As Lizzie celebrated her ninth birthday, Delcy sensed the struggle for Master Lloyd and Miss Sarah to provide for the sharecroppers and their families as they once did. Delcy and Neut needed more space to care for a growing family.

Later that year, in the early spring while Neut was planting the tobacco crop, Master Lloyd suffered a heart attack and nearly died. The tobacco barn was in need of repairs and the crops were demanding much of Neut's time. Due to the death of Pearlie, Delcy helped more with Anna, Master Lloyd and Miss Sarah. Lizzie was often left alone to care for her younger brother and sisters.

In the spring of 1880, Master Lloyd and Miss Sarah were both in poor health and most of the buildings, including the master house, were in poor condition. Since Master Lloyd and Miss Sarah's children showed little interest in the property, there were serious decisions to be made regarding the future of the plantation. Delcy and Neut were expecting again in November, so this was a serious time in their lives to make decisions that would be in the best interest of their family.

CHAPTER 11—1880: THE YEAR OF CHANGE AND DECISION

The year 1880 began with Delcy, Neut, Lizzie, Charlie, Mary, and Martha all living in the little one room log cabin. The curtains hanging from the one window in the kitchen were always freshly starched and crisp. A patch quilt hanging from the ceiling beam served as a room divider, separating the sleeping quarters of Delcy and Neut from that of the four children. Lizzie, Mary and Martha shared one big mattress on the floor near the potbellied stove. The overstuffed straw mattress always had colorful quilts made from scraps that Miss Sarah had passed on to Delcy. Charlie had his own mattress. He did not mind sleeping alone since Martha, the youngest of the children, often wet the bed.

Every morning Delcy would hang the quilts out to dry. Neut made his way to the fields and Lizzie helped the children get dressed and prepared breakfast. Chores were done around the log cabin before leaving for the Sheff house. One spring morning, Delcy was hesitant about attending to her chores at the masters' house. She was "free"; no longer a slave, yet she still acted and felt like one. She was no further ahead in her life at age 26 than she was at age 16 when she met Neut ten years ago. She always wanted her own home, a place where her children could truly be free of the ways of slavery. She thought long and hard how she still addressed Lloyd Sheff as "Master Lloyd" and Sarah Sheff as "Miss Sarah". Her children deserved more than the continued struggle and mental anguish of slavery. Delcy thought about how it could be if she were allowed to make her own decisions.

Despite occasional failures and feelings of despair, she knew that she and Neut could make it on their own. She could see the gradual decline of Master Lloyd and Miss Sarah. She knew time was closing in on their life and their ability to maintain the plantation. For the remainder of the day, all Delcy could think about was a way off the plantation. If they were ever to make a move, it was now, right after the crops were planted. Charlie was growing larger and stronger every day. Delcy knew he would soon be old enough to work the fields behind a team of mules. She certainly did not want to see him working for Master Lloyd.

The time seemed right for Delcy to look beyond the plantation. Lizzie was tiring of the household routine of cleaning and feeding Anna, who was still locked in the third floor room. It was hard for Lizzie to help Delcy care for Mary and Martha, look after the farm animals, help with the family meals, and occasionally tend to old Miss Sarah. Delcy was definitely getting impatient with caring for everyone but herself.

The year 1880 did indeed prove to be a time of decisions. Delcy could hardly wait for Neut to return home from the fields so she could vent her frustrations about living on the plantation. She was ready to put her foot down and let him know that it was time to move on. She reminded Neut that he was doing the work of two or three people. When he would return to the cabin after a long day of work, he was so tired that often he would rely on Charlie and Lizzie to do more of the hauling of water and splitting the wood for the old worn-out cook stove at the Sheff's house, as well as for their family. In the past, when field help was living on the plantation, chores were often divided, but now the free blacks did not return to Master Lloyd's fields. They left looking for the promise of land, seed, and a mule. However, Delcy doubted if they ever found that dream, but she was not looking for a dream, she only wanted a chance to earn wages for her work.

She was a beautiful laundress, and on several occasions she had done laundry for other plantation owners. Some lived as far as Georgetown, a little village about 30 miles from the Sheff plantation. She could place three irons on a hot stove at once and turn out a beautiful load of clothes. Delcy was also a good cook and there wasn't much she couldn't fix. She remembered how Mama Leah could always seemingly make a little bit go a long way. She could make the best fried apple pies and bread pudding from leftover bread. Because sewing was another of her skills, she often mended Neut's overalls over several sets of patches. They held up so well, they lasted another season. The children didn't have much in terms of clothes, but they were always neat and clean.

Delcy wondered about her parents and two brothers, Reuben and Josh. She imagined if they were still alive, and if so, how they looked.

When Neut returned from the fields and his evening chores were done, Delcy had prepared a special meal that included leftovers from Master Lloyd and Miss Sarah's supper. The children were playing outside the cabin, unaware that Mama Delcy had a verbal surprise for

Neut. When Neut came in for supper, Delcy did not hesitate in telling him that she was prepared to leave the plantation "right now!." Neut was taken by the sudden and firm voice of Delcy. He listened carefully as Delcy put forth her best argument.

"Neut," she said,

"You still act like a slave." "Yes sir Master this and yes sir Master that, you are so beholding to Master Lloyd."

Neut knew Delcy was serious. She snapped her eyes and put her hands on her hips in exhibiting a temper that Neut had not seen in her for a long time. She was making her point, that it was time to begin their move off the plantation into a land where free people could earn money for their labor. Master Lloyd's tobacco crop was so small that he barely made enough to keep food on his table, which meant even less for Neut and his family.

She discussed with Neut the possibility of getting hired as a sharecropper on another farm where the crops were being planted. All day Neut thought about the outburst of Delcy. He knew she would accept no excuse to stay. Several days later, Neut decided to take a trip to look for another sharecropping job and a better place to move his family. The plans to leave the plantation were finally in motion. He hooked the team of mules to the wagon and sat squarely on the wood wagon seat as he had done many times. He dared not look back for fear he would change his mind. After all, there were other free blacks seeking jobs and Neut feared that he would not be hired.

After several weeks of promises and looking for a piece of land and a house he could fix up for his family, he met Mr. Walters, a tobacco farmer near Georgetown. Neut was inquiring about work at the general store in Georgetown when Les Snider, the store owner, told him he knew a farmer named Stewart Walters who was looking for help to sharecrop on his tobacco farm. He gave Neut the directions to Mr. Walters' farm that was about five miles from Georgetown. Neut thanked Mr. Snider and boarded his wagon headed for the Walters' farm. As he entered the farm from the main road, Mr. Walters was fixing a gate near the entrance to the farm. He greeted Neut with a pleasant handshake and said,

"Could I help you?"

Neut mentioned that Mr. Snider, the general store owner, had told him that he might find work on his farm. Mr. Walters welcomed Neut and invited him to get off the wagon and join him on the porch where they could talk. Neut was hopeful that Mr. Walters would hire him. Neut could tell the farm had been kept up and everything was neat and trimmed.

Mr. Walters was glad to hire a strong honest worker. He promised Neut that he would sell him one acre of land at the far north corner of the farm that had an abandoned log cabin on it as well as an out house and a fenced in chicken coop for fifty dollars, if he would work for him for five years. This sounded like a fair deal to Neut.

The two rode on the wagon to see the land and the old log cabin. Even though it was in bad condition, it could be repaired over time. The promising thing about the old log cabin was that it could be enlarged so the children could have room for beds, and they would not have to sleep on the floor, especially during the cold, harsh winter months. Mr. Walters told Neut that he could have the wood from an old corncrib that had been torn down to make room for a new barn. Because Neut was handy around the farm, he was always fixing things for Master Lloyd and Miss Sarah, so he was confident he could make the cabin larger for his family. Neut and Mr. Walters shook hands and Neut got back on the wagon, gave the mules a snap of the reins and drove the thirty miles back to the Sheff plantation. He was so excited that he could hardly wait to tell Delcy the good news. All the way back he thought about adding a little cooking area for Delcy, and maybe a washing house next to the cabin; and raising chickens, and planting a garden. The children would be free to run and play and help with the garden and care for the animals. Delcy could take in laundry just like she planned in order to earn extra money to help with the children. As he approached the Sheff plantation, he urged the mules to move a little faster. He knew that Delcy would be very happy to hear of his successful trip.

Once home, Delcy ran to meet Neut as he stepped of the wagon. Delcy asked,

"Good news, I hope?"

When Neut told Delcy the story of moving to a new farm with the dream of a home and an acre of land, Delcy danced and sang for joy. The children huddled around as Delcy and Neut started praising God and jumping up and down. Martha, the youngest, was turning five months old, and Lizzie, now ten, always paid attention to Mary and Charlie so they would not get into trouble. They were too young, of course, to understand the meaning of what was happening. Lizzie

75

understood somewhat, but seemed confused and uncertain. That evening, the news of moving and having a home of their own was overwhelming. The happy event called for a special celebration. Delcy fixed one of her special suppers. She had saved vegetables and meat from the Sheff's cellar and smoke house for just such an occasion.

Delcy noticed that Lizzie appeared sad. Charlie and Mary were singing and dancing along with Neut and Delcy while Lizzie held baby Martha gently comforting her during the excitement and celebration. Mama Delcy sat in the rocker and pulled Lizzie up on her knee and explained to her what she felt it would be like to be free. She explained that as long as they stayed on Master Lloyd and Miss Sarah's plantation, they would never be free. They would always be treated as slaves, beholding to the Sheff's whims and needs with no dignity or respect. Lizzie was thinking about the friendship with Lucy, the Sheff's oldest granddaughter. She was her only friend. When Lucy would visit Grandma and Grandpa Sheff she would always play school with Lizzie and bring her a book to read. Lizzie was always excited to see Lucy and hear about her school in Georgetown. Lizzie believed that someday she would be able to go to school. It was a good thought but one Lizzie knew was far in the distance and a journey all in itself. Caring for the children and helping Mama Delcy came before anything.

Charlie had mixed feelings about moving. This was the only place he had ever known. In fact, he had only been off the plantation twice in his life, and that was when Neut took him to a neighboring plantation to pick up grain for the animals. Charlie did not have much time to play like most eight-year-old boys. He often got to ride the mules home from the field to the Master's house. He enjoyed talking to them as he was giving them food and water. Sometimes he played with the three Sheff grandsons. He didn't care much for Jebb who was somewhat of a bully. He often teased Charlie about how black his color was, and how white Lizzie was. One time Jebb made a remark about Lizzie being half white and that Grandpa Sheff was her "pappy." Charlie got so mad he hit Jebb with all his might and they rolled and tumbled on the dusty ground until Charlie pinned him down. He gave Jebb a good licking and made him say "Uncle" and also promise to never say anything like that again. Delcy made Charlie go home and scolded Jebb for starting the fight. She had explained to Lizzie why her color was different from that of Charlie, Mary and Martha. Lizzie accepted Master Lloyd as her father, but not in the loving and compassionate way she accepted Neut. After all, Delcy had married Neut when Lizzie was barely a year old. Neut was the only father Lizzie knew and loved.

After the planting of the spring tobacco crop in late May, Neut and Delcy broke the news to Master Lloyd and Miss Sarah that they would be moving to their own land and home in Georgetown where Mr. Walters, a tobacco farmer, had sold them an acre of land. They were looking forward to the promise of a better life for their family. Master Lloyd, Miss Sarah, and Anna would have to turn to their children for help. Master Lloyd was very ill and slowly dying from internal bleeding. Neut had made an agreement with Mr. Walters that they would prepare to move in about a month, giving the Sheff children time to make arrangements for the care of their parents and Anna.

CHAPTER 12—1880: TRAGEDY ON THE PLANTATION

Neut, Delcy, and the children began to make plans to leave the Sheff plantation within the next few weeks. In the meanwhile, after a long and agonizing illness of the "flux", which resulted in bleeding of the bowels, Master Lloyd died. Poor old Miss Sarah, partially paralyzed, was as "nutty as a fruitcake" and could not be left alone. She could not be trusted to do anything without someone watching or helping her. At the death of master Lloyd, Delcy figured the Sheff children would move quickly to bury him in the family cemetery located on the plantation. The children also had to decide what to do with Miss Sarah and Anna. As Delcy and Neut attended the burial of master Lloyd, the Sheff family was apparently anxious to settle the estate and put Miss Sarah in a "feeble minded" institution where she could live the rest of her life. Anna was the most difficult to decide the best placement for. After all, she had never been beyond the walls of the Sheff house. Since she was blind and unable to move about, her care was more demanding than Miss Sarah. The Sheff children had very little time to make decisions for their family before Neut, Delcy, and the children would be moving.

None of the children or grandchildren showed any interest in the tobacco plantation. As a gesture of good will and loyalty, the children offered Neut and Delcy the team of mules and wagon along with their belongings in the cabin. Neut inquired about taking some of the food in the cellar and smoke house and a small assortment of tools that would help him fix up his new home. All the Sheff children agreed that Neut and Delcy were indeed deserving, and offered to share other small items from the Sheff's house. Neut and Delcy quickly removed the items offered them and returned to the log cabin.

As the Sheff children prepared to pack the necessary clothes and personal items for Miss Sarah and Anna, they noticed smoke coming from the kitchen area of the house. The children scurried around trying to locate the smell of smoke. It didn't take long to discover that the old kitchen stove had burning cinders falling on the wooden floor under the stove. The flames had already spread under the sink and had set fire to the icebox sitting in the corner. Without warning, the kitchen curtains went up in flames. The curtains and wallpaper began to burn fiercely. The most anyone could do was save their lives and that of Miss Sarah and Anna.

The children began frantically to try to reach Anna on the third floor as the flames roared from room to room. No one could find the key to unlock the door and the smoke and heat was so intense that the locked door could not be approached to save Anna.

As the family ran from the burning house, Neut, Delcy and the children could see the masters' house burning from a distance. By the time they returnd to the Sheff home it was fully engulfed in flames. Everything was lost. Anna never had a chance. Miss Sarah began to mumble about Anna in the locked room. She had tried to enter the burning house but the children restrained her. After the flames died down, Anna's charred body was removed from the house and buried next to master Lloyd. As the children were preparing Miss Sarah to leave, the key to the attic was found in a little pocket purse that she kept in her dress pocket. The family grieved openly at the tragic death of Anna.

Neut and Delcy felt mixed emotions at the burning of what was once a grand home for the Sheff family. Neut's feelings were far more sympathetic than Delcy's. Her sadness was tempered by a feeling of relief, and a sense of justice for all the harsh treatment, pain, and injustice the Sheff's had wrought upon her. The Sheff children led Miss Sarah to the wagon where some of her belongings were packed in an old trunk that had been stored in the barn. As the Sheff family yelled a "giddy-up" to the team of horses pulling the wagon, Miss Sarah looked back and began to weep quietly, knowing that she would never return to the plantation life and lifestyle to which she had become accustomed. But mostly she felt the horror of Anna's death that would haunt her forever.

Neut, Delcy and the children watched as the wagon carrying Miss Sarah left the plantation. They were saddened by the horrible death of Anna but excited to have a place to move to that would belong to them. Finally, a place they could call home. As the children helped with the final packing of the furniture in the cabin and collecting the tools, there was barely enough room for them. Neut and Delcy rearranged some of the things on the wagon to make room for the final item in the cabin, the old pecan wood rocking chair. The old chair was needed to rock the next baby that Neut and Delcy were expecting.

Lizzie sighed as she squeezed between the furniture, holding Martha in her lap to keep her from bouncing around. Delcy and Neut sat proudly together on the wooden bench attached to the wagon. Neut gave the mules a snap of the whip and moved toward the path that led past the burned home and onto the open road that led to Georgetown. As the wagon rolled past familiar things on the plantation, such as the duck and chicken pen, and the stall where the old red cow was milked, Lizzie began to softly cry.

Delcy sat quietly on the wooden wagon bench reflecting on her life of abuse, punishment, the selling of her parents, the loss of her brothers, the birth of Lizzie, and finally the marriage to Neut. From the time of her birth in 1854 to the present time of June 1, 1880 was an experience in life that she never wanted her children to have to suffer through. She explained to Lizzie that she never wanted her to experience not having a loving mother and father, and always being at the mercy of a brutal and sexually abusive master. Lizzie listened and tried to understand. She asked Mama Delcy to tell her about where they were going. Delcy told her it was a better place and someday they would understand how much it meant to have something that's ours. Lizzie asked about going to school, and if there would be friends to play with. Delcy promised her that she would be able to go to school, maybe not every day, but she would continue to learn to read and write, so she could teach Charlie and the other children.

As the wagon rolled out into the open space of the fields and trees, the children became more thrilled. They had only been off the plantation once or twice in their lives. As the view of the property grew smaller and smaller in a haze of dust kicked up by the rolling wobbly wagon wheels, Lizzie waved her little hand to the land in the distance. The journey was beginning; it was a point of no return. Neut snapped the reins of the mules; their new home was just a few miles away.

CHAPTER 13—1880: THE SUMMER - A NEW DESTINY

Traveling from the Sheff plantation to the farm of Mister Walters near Georgetown was a distance of about thirty miles. Leaving the Sheff's place was a cross roads in their lives; they were shaking off the mental and physical shackles of slavery and taking on a new life of freedom. Delcy's dream of freedom was finally a reality. She could hardly wait to attend a real African Methodist Church and make friends and listen to a preacher talk about freedom and read the Bible. She knew there was a school in Georgetown for African American children. They called it the Freedom School. She did not know much about city living. The only time she ever left the plantation was to attend a funeral with Miss Sarah on an adjoining plantation. She hoped so much that Charlie, Lizzie and Mary could go to school regularly. She dreamed of loading the children in the wagon and driving the five miles to Georgetown where she could look at pretty clothes in the store windows. If she could earn enough money from her washing and ironing, she could buy material to make the children's clothes and perhaps new curtains. Most of all, she wanted the children to have new shoes that fit. She knew that very soon she would be truly free, and nobody would ever treat her like a slave or take her joy of freedom. She wondered what Neut was thinking. Once she saw him looking back as though he was afraid of what lay ahead. She gently placed her hand on his sturdy shoulder and assured him that the journey to their new home would be their first step of hope for a better life.

Lizzie held on to Martha as the wagon bumped and squeaked along the road across the miles to the new farm. As the evening sun began to set, the wagon loaded with all their belongings rolled onto the Walters farm. Even though the trip had taken all day, the children were excited and full of energy. They wanted to see as much of the new farm as possible before the sun set. As the wagon stopped in front of Mr. Walters' home, he came out to meet Neut, Delcy, and the children. He directed them toward the acre of land that housed the log cabin, long ago abandoned by the slaves. Neut guided the wagon down the rutted path for the last quarter mile to what would be their new home.

As Neut halted the wagon in front of the cabin, Delcy and the children anxiously hopped off the wagon, eager to examine their new home. As Delcy pushed open the door, she and the children slowly entered the log cabin expecting the worst. It was empty except for a cooking stove Mr. Walters had moved into the cabin. He also had left a few cooking utensils on the kitchen sink along with an old oil lamp full of oil.

Delcy was excited. As Neut and the children started unloading the wagon, Delcy made a fire in the stove, using wood from a small pile outside. She prepared some of the food that was given her from the cellar of the Sheff plantation. The children were allowed to run and play. They were so tired that they barely ate the stewed vegetables and salt pork Delcy had prepared. After supper, Lizzie and Charlie set up the mattresses and covered them with big fluffy quilts. As they prepared to bed down for the night, Neut offered a prayer of thanksgiving for their new home and a new start as a truly free family.

The next day Mr. Walters rode his mare down to the cabin and offered other small household items to the family. Delcy was very thankful and asked Mr. Walters about working in the house and what was expected of her and the children. She did not hesitate to let him know that she was expecting another child in the spring of 1881, and that she would like some type of wage for her service. She felt good about letting him know right up front that she was a free woman.

She asked him about taking in washing and ironing and having Sunday off so she and the family could go to church. She was also concerned that Lizzie should have some kind of schooling so she could teach the other children to read and write. He told Delcy that there was a school for "colored" children in Georgetown, and he was sure she could have Sunday off. In fact, he thought that taking in washing and ironing would be helpful for her to earn extra money.

Delcy had never been listened to with so much understanding and compassion. She glanced at Neut with a seriousness that took him by surprise. Delcy seemed certain of what she wanted that Mr. Walters could only agree that it was the right thing to do.

Mr. Walters told Delcy about his family and what he expected of her in the house. He admitted to Delcy that he needed someone to help with the care of his wife, who had been sick for several years. She was bed-ridden and unable to care for herself. Delcy assured him that she would clean and prepare the meals and take daily care of his wife. Mr. Walters told her that their children helped out on Sundays and she would be able to have time with her family. That suited her just fine. So far, Mr. Walters had granted Delcy what she wanted.

After getting settled in the cabin the next day, Charlie cut wood for the stove and help Papa Neut with the farm chores while Lizzie cared for the children and dreamed of making new friends. Lizzie did not see any children her age that she could play with or help her with her reading and writing. She became quiet and appeared unsure about the new home. Delcy told Lizzie that she would be busy for a while getting adjusted to the new farm, and she was certain there would be children her age at church. Later that day, Delcy and the children made their way to the Walters' house and met Miss Liza, Mr. Walters' wife. Miss Liza seemed glad to meet Delcy and the children. Delcy could see that they would get along from the start. She was nothing like Miss Sarah.

Miss Liza was a well-schooled lady and her room was filled with books and various pictures and ornaments. As the children entered the house, they were very quiet and amazed at all the beautiful things sitting around on heavily starched doilies and table covers. Lizzie was excited about seeing all the books and beautiful pictures. She asked Miss Liza for permission to see some of her books. She modestly told Miss Liza that she could read and write a little. Miss Liza offered to teach Lizzie to read and write. She was very pleased that Lizzie could already read somewhat. Miss Liza loved having children around her. Lizzie was very polite and appreciated her kind offer to teach her. Miss Liza had become the friend that Lizzie needed to care about her.

She would be glad to help Mama Delcy at the house while Charlie watched the children so she could learn from Miss Liza. Before Lizzie left the house for the day, Miss Liza offered her a small primer book to take home. Later, that night after supper, Lizzie began to read the little book to Charlie and the family. She was extremely happy.

On Sunday, Neut and Delcy loaded all the children in the wagon and headed for church out in the country. The little African Methodist church was about ten miles from the farm. In fact, the church was located about halfway between Leesburg and Georgetown. What a joy for Delcy, Neut, and the children to be able to experience real singing and preaching. There were many children to play with. Delcy and Neut found everyone very friendly. The preacher talked about God and His son Jesus and how he wanted us to be free. After all the singing and preaching they took up a collection for the preacher. They didn't have anything to give but they believed they soon would. Excitingly, Neut and Delcy looked forward to the Sunday when they could give an offering. After church the preacher stood at the door thanking them for coming, and as he shook everyone's hand, he invited them back next Sunday. They sang all the way home. Delcy was beginning to enjoy freedom in a way that was hard to express. She spent a considerable time shouting and praising God for setting her and the family free.

In the meanwhile, Mr. Walters told several families in Georgetown about Delcy taking in washing and ironing. She had gotten permission from Mr. Walters to borrow the wagon to go into town once a week to pick up laundry, and she would return the finished clothes on the weekend. The first week, Mr. Walters lined up two families that wanted her services. At last she was earning a little money. She earned about two dollars and twenty-six cents for her first week's work. Soon the word got around that Delcy was a good laundress and all her customers were pleased. Delcy began to teach Lizzie how to iron, and soon they had enough ironing to keep them both busy.

When Lizzie would go with Delcy to work in the Walters' house, Miss Liza was always glad to see her and willingly helped her to read and write and do simple math. One day Miss Liza offered Lizzie a big storybook to take home. Lizzie could hardly finish her chores. She wanted to read the new book given to her by Miss Liza. Delcy, Neut and the children were thankful to Mr. Walters and Miss Liza for helping them with their family, and for allowing Delcy to take in ironing, and for teaching Lizzie to read and write. Neut was glad they moved to the Walters farm. He promised Delcy he would fix up the cabin before winter, and they would have a joyous celebration when the tobacco crop sold in the fall. Mr. Walters had proved to be an honest person, and Neut assured him he would honor the handshake agreement to work for five years to pay off the fifty dollars debt on the one-acre of farmland and the cabin.

As Delcy became more comfortable caring for Miss Liza, they began to confide in each other about their families. Delcy found out that Miss Liza was partially paralyzed from a previous stroke she had several years ago. Because Delcy and Lizzie were very patient with

Miss Liza, Mr. Walters often rewarded them by giving them a little extra money for her care and for their work around the house.

Charlie, Mary and Martha were very careful not to touch any of the beautiful dishes and pictures in the main house. Delcy had instructed them to never touch things that did not belong to them. The children were very attentive to Miss Liza and only entered her room when she invited them. Delcy was grateful that she could bring the children with her to work. When Charlie worked the tobacco fields with Neut, and Lizzie helped Delcy with the housework at Miss Liza's, Mary and Martha had to come along.

Lizzie continued to make progress with her studies. She had read several books and her writing and math skills were improving. Charlie, Delcy and Neut were also learning to read the Bible. Lizzie would sit in the rocker and teach Mama and Papa to read and write along with Charlie.

There was not much extra time around the farm, so right after supper, everyone would help clean the kitchen so they could have reading time. Everyone would sit around the potbellied stove to keep warm while Lizzie would read stories. Neut and Charlie were often busy with the fall harvest of the tobacco and gathering the last vegetables from the garden, thus they would sometimes work after supper and miss hearing Lizzie read.

Delcy's days were busy preparing food for storage in the cellar which included dried beans, sweet potatoes, turnips, apples and red potatoes. Delcy and Lizzie were also busy with washing and ironing which consisted of making the trip to town to pick up and drop off freshly pressed clothes for other families.

Delcy was beginning to show with her fifth child. She had been through childbirth enough times that she knew exactly what to do. Lizzie was hoping that the new baby would be a boy. She also knew that she would have to help with another baby. Lizzie wanted to continue her reading and writing lessons so that Miss Liza would let her bring more books home to read to the family. Lizzie hoped another baby would not interfere with her friendship with Miss Liza.

On Sundays, Delcy, Neut and the children were getting to know more sharecroppers from other farms. Attending church was an important time for Delcy, Neut, and the children to socialize with other families. They enjoyed going to church for the sermon and staying for the basket dinners after church. Everyone would bring a dish of their best "fixings". There would be pecan pies, fried chicken, sweet potatoes, green beans and salads. The women would spread the food from their baskets on benches and tables sometimes inside the church or outside if the weather was nice, and everyone would eat from each other's pots and pans. Delcy's favorite food to fix was fried apple pies. She knew to soak the dried apples until they were plump and juicy. She would add butter, sugar, and spices, then spread the mixture on little circles of a flaky pie crust. Then she would fry them in a big black cast iron skillet until golden brown. The fried pies were enjoyed by everyone and always seemed to be one of the most popular desserts.

As the fall winds blew and the shorter days of winter began, Neut and Charlie were busy cutting and stacking the wood beside the cabin and the air holes in the cabin were filled with mud to keep out the wind. It was another cold winter and the children were kept busy tending the animals as well as making certain Mr. Walters and Miss Liza were warm and comfortable.

Because the winter was so cold and the children were small, Delcy, Neut and the children were often unable to make the ten-mile trip to church. They really missed going to church. Most of all, they missed their friends. But with Delcy approaching her seventh month of pregnancy, it was too risky to leave during the bitterly cold months. The roads were often closed due to snowdrifts and if they could not make it home there would be little or no help on the road. This was the first winter the family had in their own home. Delcy and Neut made certain the children had a warm cozy home and, most of all, beds to sleep in rather than sleeping on the damp mud floor.

As the season changed from winter to spring, on March 18, 1881, Delcy gave birth to a son. She named him Nace. Charlie was glad to have a brother. The little sisters pitched in to help. Lizzie began her usual care of the new baby rocking him to sleep in the rocking chair. She was a good big sister, very loving and patient when caring for the children. As the early spring season neared, life for Neut, Delcy and the children was never better. They had survived the long cold winter with plenty food and a warm cabin. The little log cabin was filled with laughter and singing. Neut and Mr. Walters walked around the farm to make plans for the spring planting. Neut was counting the time until he would own his acre of land- only four more years to go.

As Neut, Charlie and Mr. Walters prepared the tobacco fields, Neut made certain the equipment was in good shape and the mules ready to go. Between the years 1881 and 1883 the family was able to earn more than enough money to pay Mr. Walters the fifty dollars for the one acre of farmland. In fact, they had saved enough to remodel the old log cabin. Another bedroom was added, the washroom was enlarged and a porch was built on the front. Delcy would soon need the space. She had given birth to her seventh child September 19, 1883 – a boy she named Benjamin. The farm prospered and Mr. Walters always paid Neut his fair share of the tobacco crop when it was sold on the market. Neut and Mr. Walters had a gentleman's agreement that made them more than boss and sharecropper – they respected each other as friends.

In the spring of 1886 Miss Liza's health began to fail and she became less able to help Lizzie with her studies. Lizzie had a good start that enabled her to teach her brothers and sisters how to read and write. One Sunday morning in May 1886 Miss Liza died in her sleep. Mr. Walters was now alone. His life seemed empty. Life was not the same with Miss Liza gone. Shortly after the funeral on May 17, 1886 Delcy gave birth to her eighth child, a boy, John Eli. She called him Eli after her father.

Mr. Walters, Neut and the children continued to work the farm for many years. The Walter's children and grand children continued to visit their father on Sunday and they too established a friendship with

Clarice Boswell

the Smith family. Mr. Walters died in 1892 after a short illness. His elder son, Jacob, continued to run the farm after the death of his father.

CHAPTER 14—1885: LIZZIE'S JOURNEY

Lizzie, now fifteen, was interested in meeting friends at the Leesburg Methodist Church and maybe even going to a candy 'taffy pull' or a Saturday night social occasionally. Neut agreed to take her and Charlie on some Saturday evenings after all the chores were done. It was during one of the church socials that she met a young man named James (Jim) Davis. Lizzie knew she was too young to be serious about a young man, but she did enjoy his company. Lizzie thought about marriage, but she knew she was needed to help care for the small children as well as help with the household chores at the Walters home.

Lizzie and Jim started seeing each other more often. Two years later, when Lizzie turned seventeen, Jim asked her to marry him and move to Georgetown where he lived and sharecropped on another farm. The idea of marriage literally swept Lizzie off her feet. First, this was a way out of an overcrowded cabin where the family was steadily growing and space was scarce. Also, the idea of living in Georgetown really appealed to her. Lizzie had only left the farm to go with Delcy to pick up laundry and to church at Leesburg. Jim asked Neut and Delcy for Lizzie's hand in marriage and in 1887, Lizzie and Jim Davis were married in a simple ceremony at the Leesburg Methodist Church. There was no honeymoon. Lizzie packed up a few things from the family cabin and moved from the farm to a little house in Georgetown adjoining the farm where Jim was a sharecropper. Lizzie was very excited to have her own little house.

She fixed up the house and made it home for Jim and herself. She knew several people in Georgetown, since over the past seven years they had done laundry for many families. Lizzie made her way around the town looking for other people interested in hiring her to do their laundry. Over a period of several months, Lizzie had a half dozen customers that she laundered for every week. She earned enough to keep the household going and put a few dollars away for the baby she was expecting the next year in July. Jim and Lizzie were excited about the new baby.

Lizzie could hardly wait to see Mama Delcy, Papa Neut, and the children on Sunday at church so she could tell them the good news. Lizzie worked up until the time she gave birth to her first son, William Aaron, born, July 31, 1889. Lizzie was a loving and caring mother to her baby son. After all, Lizzie was accustomed to caring for babies. She had practically raised the first seven babies that Delcy and Neut had. As soon as Lizzie got her strength back, she worked in the home taking in laundry, baking pastries, and doing alterations on clothes. Lizzie even sold vegetables from the little garden that she had planted at the back of the house. She did a variety of things to keep the family going financially.

Two years after the birth of Will, Lizzie gave birth to a baby girl whom she named Leah, after Delcy's mother, the grandmother she never knew. Lizzie found that two babies were a handful. It was becoming a problem for Lizzie that Jim was not home very often. She spent an increasing amount of time alone with the children. One Sunday, while attending church, Lizzie overheard the ladies talking about Jim and some of the things he was doing. This caused Lizzie to become suspicious about his absence from the home. As the year ended and the tobacco crop was sold, Lizzie noticed that Jim was unwilling to share his profit from the sale of tobacco with her and the children. As time passed, their marriage became strained. Lizzie tried to keep the marriage and family together. Feeling very distraught, Lizzie was pregnant with their third child.

The year 1893, Lizzie gave birth to a son she named Charlie, after her beloved brother. Lizzie was beginning to suffer from hard times, both financially and spiritually. It was hard to keep up with her many odd jobs and manage three small children. Lizzie soon realized that Jim was no longer faithful to her and the children. Her dilemma was what to do. She knew she could not go back home to Delcy and Neut, because there were now nine children in the Smith home and space was not adequate to bring three more babies to an already overcrowded home.

As winter approached, Lizzie formally divorced Jim Davis in the year 1895. There she was with three small children: Will, six, Leah, four, and Charlie, barely two. Lizzie pondered her situation. She knew she had to leave the little house she had worked so hard to fix up, but she needed a safe place for the children. She had become acquainted with many people in Georgetown and she knew there had to be a family that would take them in for labor and minimal wages. She knew Mrs. Opel Smothers was a good and kindhearted person who had a servant's home that was not in use. Lizzie recalled that once when she was about fifteen, Mrs. Smothers had asked her if she wanted to live in her home and work for her. At that time, Lizzie could not because she was needed at home to help Mama Delcy with the children and attend to the farm. Now, more than ever she needed to know if the offer still stood.

Lizzie and the three children bundled up and walked the short distance to Mrs. Smothers home to inquire about working for her and staying in the servant's house. Mrs. Smothers, who knew that Lizzie was an honest, hard-working woman, agreed that Lizzie and the family could move in as soon as the house could be cleaned since it had not been used for several years. The next few days Lizzie and the children returned to clean the little house. The day before Thanksgiving, they moved in and Lizzie began work for the Smothers family. Mrs. Smothers was very generous to Lizzie and the children. They always had plenty food, milk, bread and fresh churned butter. Lizzie felt very blessed to have such a safe place to live. Lizzie was given scraps of fabric to make clothes for the children and quilts for their beds. Once a month Mrs. Smothers would allow Lizzie to use the family wagon and horse to visit her family in Georgetown and go to church. She was always glad to see Mama Delcy and Papa Neut. She always marveled at how her brothers and sisters had grown and how excited they were to see her.

Lizzie worked for the Smothers family for three years before meeting her second husband, Simon Cannon, who was a widower with an infant daughter. His wife had died as a result of giving birth to their daughter, Annie Bell, born February 22, 1896. Lizzie was very cautious in accepting Simon's attention. She was hesitant about keeping company with any man, and certainly had not contemplated re-marrying so soon. Simon asked Lizzie if she would consider helping with the care of his infant daughter Annie Bell. Lizzie agreed to help with her care while working for the Smothers family. Annie Bell was no problem to care for, and her daughter, Leah, was excited to have a baby in the house. Mrs. Smothers did not mind Lizzie adding one more child to the family. Lizzie eventually got to know Simon as an honest and caring person, and a relationship began that would eventually lead to marriage.

Simon was a very successful farmer who sharecropped on a big tobacco farm outside Georgetown. He was offered a chance to sharecrop and become the overseer of a larger tobacco farm in Jessamine County, Kentucky. Sharecropping a larger farm would enable Simon to make more money, and it would also give Lizzie's three children a chance to work the fields to earn money. On the farm in Jessamine County there was a little house on the property that was once used as a trolley car station for passengers going between Nicholasville and Lexington, Kentucky. The little station was called the tollgate house. Even though it was small, it was in good condition and could easily be converted to a home for Lizzie and the children. After two years of courtship, Lizzie consented to marry Simon on November 12, 1898. Lizzie, Annie Bell, Will, Leah, and Charlie packed up their belongings from the Smothers house and moved to their new home located near the side of the road in Nicholasville, Kentucky. The old tollgate house was now a home for the Simon Cannon family.

Once again Lizzie and the children fixed up the little place and added fresh curtains and new fluffy quilts to the beds, which made it home. It was not hard to find work in Nicholasville. Lizzie quickly got out the word that she would take in laundry and was available to clean houses. Many residents from Nicholasville would drive by the house and drop off their laundry and alterations. Lizzie and Leah were in business. Everyone helped with the field crops as well as the household chores. Simon was a good stepfather to Lizzie's three children as well as a good father to Annie Bell. He truly adored his new wife Lizzie, and was always concerned about her well-being. What a change from her first marriage to Jim Davis. Lizzie had to learn to trust all over again. Because she had waited three years before accepting Simon's hand in marriage, she had an appreciation of what marriage and family life should be. After settling into their home and getting to know people in the little community of Nicholasville, Simon and Lizzie moved their church membership from the Leesburg Methodist Church to Bethel African Methodist Episcopal Church in Nicholasville. Lizzie, Simon and the children became active members in the Sunday school. Simon joined the Board of Trustees and Lizzie became a member of the Missionary society of the church. The little church on the corner of York Avenue was in need of repair and expansion to accommodate the increasing membership. Simon was a very active financial member and was one of several trustees to sign a loan to help remodel and expand the church. After several months of marriage, Lizzie and Simon began their family.

The year 1900, May 15, Lizzie gave birth to a son named Elmer. Elmer was a difficult birth and was born with serious health problems. He lived a little more than four months. He died October 4, 1900 from pneumonia. The death of Elmer was devastating to the mental health of Lizzie. In despair, she confided in Mama Delcy and found strength in her support. Also, in the year 1900, at the age of forty-six, Delcy gave birth to her thirteenth and last child. Delcy reminded Lizzie that she had four children to die before age three. She knew how heart breaking it was to see one's babies die so young. Lizzie found comfort in the fact that she had a family that supported her during this difficult time. Lizzie was a woman of great faith and she relied on her spiritual strength to sustain her.

She soon began helping out in the fields, working in her garden, and caring for the farm animals that Simon had purchased. Their little farm consisted of chickens, ducks, pigs, cows and several teams of mules. Every fall Simon would butcher a hog so the family would have meat for the winter. He would share the meat with Delcy and Neut when they would visit each other in Georgetown.

Two years after the death of Elmer, Lizzie was expecting another child. On January 13, 1902, Lizzie gave birth to a son they named Joe. He was a healthy baby that the family loved from the first sight. Leah, now eleven, was an affectionate big sister and was very helpful with the baby. She also was a big help to Lizzie, working in the garden and milking the cows.

Will, now thirteen was working in the fields beside Simon. Charlie, now nine, would tag along to care for the animals and haul water for the tobacco workers. After a long day of working in the tobacco fields, the children all pitched in to split wood and haul water from the spring so Lizzie and the family could have fresh drinking water everyday.

On July 30, 1904, Lizzie gave birth to another son, named Roy. Once again, this was a difficult delivery for Lizzie. When Roy was born, he had problems breathing and appeared to have seizures (probably epilepsy) that caused him to collapse and shake uncontrollably. After a constant battle of poor health, Roy died at the age of two in 1906. His death had an even greater effect, both physically and mentally, on Lizzie and Simon. Lizzie became very despondent and required a great deal of understanding and patience from her family. It was seven years before Lizzie would give birth to another child.

On March 10, 1911, Lizzie gave birth to her first daughter by Simon. They named her Mary Antionette. What a joy to give birth to a healthy baby girl. Everyone was excited. With Annie Bell now fifteen, Joe nine, and Leah, Will, and Charlie grown, the attention Mary Antionette received was constant.

Leah was now dating Frank Strauss, a much sought after gentleman and a very successful farmer in Jessamine County. He owned his own home and farm on the Shun Road in Nicholasville, Kentucky. He took a great deal of time in selecting the right woman to marry. Leah always hoped that someday she would marry Frank. However, she was very reserved and responsible as they planned their future together. She was pleased when Frank presented her with an engagement ring that properly announced his intentions to marry her.

The year 1913 was a year of joy for the family. Charlie met his wife Celia Sanders in Nicholasville, and on February 5, 1913 they were married. A few months later, Annie Bell met Willie Howard. They were married on April 16, 1913. This meant that within a few months, two of Lizzie and Simon's children moved from the home. However, Leah and Will, still single, continued to work with Simon in the tobacco fields.

Later that year, Lizzie gave birth to her last child, a son, born August 8, 1913. She named him Frank Robert. He was a real delight to older sister Mary Antionette, now two, who loved him from the first moment he was born. Leah became a second mother to the two young children while Lizzie continued to work the fields and tend to the garden and livestock. Between Leah and Lizzie, the children were always under good care.

The following year, tragedy struck the family again. In March 1914, Annie Bell died giving birth to her first child. The baby died a few days later causing great pain to the family. Simon had lost his first daughter along with his first grandchild. It seemed that death was a frequent and painful part of life. Surely, times would get better as they moved into the year 1915.

But this was not the case. Early in the spring of 1915, Joe became ill with uncontrollable coughing spells, and later began to cough up blood. He was diagnosed with tuberculosis and after a few months, he died on September 17, 1915. With his death, Lizzie had lost her first three sons by Simon.

Leah was there to support her mother. She helped with Mary Antionette and Frank Robert as though they were her own children. Lizzie had endured so much pain and loss. She continued to draw upon her strong faith and belief in God, which helped her through the difficult times.

Lizzie continued to visit her family in Georgetown as often as possible. With the crops and farm work, it was difficult to travel long distances for more than a day. On Lizzie's most recent visit to the family in Georgetown, Neut had not been feeling well. He complained of being short of breath and Lizzie noticed that his feet and hands were swollen.

In the months that followed, Neut's health continued to decline. One evening while sitting in the old pecan rocking chair, Neut had a massive heart failure and died October 30, 1916. Delcy felt a great loss in her life. Neut had been responsible for making her dream of freedom and owing a home a reality. With young children in the home, Delcy was able to continue living on the farm until the children were grown and on their own. Mary, one of the older daughters remained on the farm with Delcy.

The year 1916 was a financially bountiful year for the Cannon family. Will, Charlie, and Simon each earned nearly five hundred dollars from the sale of their tobacco crop. One more year and they would be able to purchase the farm for sale about four miles north of their home that had thirty-six acres. The property also had an old log cabin that once served as a halfway house for slaves and masters as they journeyed from the north to the south. The masters would stop there for rest and chain the slaves in a holding pen that was directly behind the cabin until such time as the master's pleasures were met, and then they moved on. Also on the farm, was an underground root cellar used to store vegetables, ice, and perishable foods such as milk and butter. The asking price for the farm was nine thousand dollars. Simon did not have enough money saved to buy the entire thirty-six acres, so he, Charlie, and Will made an agreement to purchase the farm as equal partners. They would split the farm into three plots so they each could have an equal share to raise their own tobacco crops.

In the year 1917, Leah and Frank Strauss married and Leah moved from the home to live with Frank on a farm that he owned south of Nicholasville on Shun Road. Lizzie missed her terribly. They were not only mother and daughter, but also best friends. After the marriage of Leah, Will and Charlie continued sharecropping with their stepfather, Simon, and saving their money for a down payment on the farm.

The year 1917 was another good year financially for Simon, Will, and Charlie, with the tobacco selling at a record price. With their share of the sale of the crop, they each had the necessary money to buy their twelve acres. Charlie, who was now married to Celia and living in Nicholasville, offered his twelve acres to Leah and Frank Strauss. Leah wanted to be closer to Lizzie so she could help with the family. She persuaded Frank Strauss to sell the farm on Shun Road and reinvest in the thirty-six acres with Simon and Will. It was a good buy for Leah and Frank because the farm on Shun road only had four acres.

Simon wanted the twelve acres adjoining a farm to the North of Leah and Frank. Since Leah and Frank had the largest investment to put down on their share, they chose the strip of land with the log cabin, root cellar, and tobacco barn with the understanding that Lizzie and Simon, along with Will, Mary Antionette, and Frank Robert, could live with them until the big house on the hill was finished. The big house on the hill was the home that Simon had promised to build for Lizzie and the children. Will chose to live with Simon and Lizzie and did not build a home on his property. Will was satisfied with the end strip that had an old corncrib on it that was used to store corn and hay for the cattle.

When the family moved from the old tollgate house to their new farm, the move was a boost to Lizzie's mental and emotional health. The land had several ponds and a fresh water spring that provided water for the family. A deep well was located on Leah and Frank's property that had the coldest, purest water one could imagine. In the spring of 1918, after Simon finished the home, Lizzie and the children excitedly moved in.

Simon, Will, Frank, and Leah began to purchase livestock for milk and butter, and chickens and ducks for eggs and meat. They continued to slaughter several hogs every winter, and made their own sausage and smoked their own meat in a smoke house that was built behind the big house on the hill. Lizzie and Simon began to prosper. Leah and Lizzie worked hard taking in laundry along with picking and canning vegetables from the garden. They had become a team, as they sold butter, cream, eggs, and vegetables to the stores in Nicholasville. They also participated in an open vegetable market in Nicholasville during the summer. Between working in the fields and looking after the children, they had a full day.

As the years passed, Lizzie continued to stay in touch with her family in Georgetown. She and her brother Charlie visited each other on occasion, and once a year they would have a big family reunion where all the brothers and sisters would come together and share stories about their lives and families.

By the year 1926, Delcy, now seventy-two, was beginning to fail. She had severe arthritis and she was in constant pain. Her life was gradually slowing to the extent that some days she hardly had the energy to get out of bed. All of Delcy's children were gone except for her daughter Mary. She and Delcy remained in the original cabin located on the Walters farm until Delcy's death on April 6, 1926. Lizzie and the family attended the funeral that was held at the Leesburg Methodist Church where she and Neut and the children were members. Delcy was laid to rest in the church cemetery next to Neut.

Mary remained in the old home less than a year. It was in need of repair and more than Mary could care for by herself. Mary offered to divide the few belongings in the cabin among the brothers and sisters. All Lizzie wanted was the old pecan rocking chair that was part of the original furniture when her grand parents, Leah and Eli, moved into the log cabin on the Sheff plantation in 1850, and the family Bible dating back to 1876. Granny Delcy, as she was affectionately called, would have wanted Lizzie, her first born, to have the old rocking chair and the Bible as a memento of the past life that once existed on the plantation.

Lizzie placed the pecan rocker in a special place in the big house on the hill. It was in need of repair, but the spirit of those from the past remained alive in the old chair. With the death of both parents, Lizzie felt blessed to have a home, a loving husband and five living children; Will, Leah, Charlie, Mary Antionette, and Frank Robert.

Lizzie turned her attention to providing an education for Mary Antionette and Frank Robert. They had been attending a small rural "colored" school called Little Zion that housed the first through eighth grade. Contrary to the customary educational goals for most blacks at the time, Lizzie had bigger plans for their continued education past the eighth grade. She visited the school in Nicholasville for "colored" children and met Professor Caldwell who was eager to enroll them in a high school program. Throughout Jessamine County there were several rural schools that offered the "colored" children an opportunity to learn to read and write, though most only went through the eighth grade. However, most "colored" children were occupied with working the tobacco fields, and school was not a high priority for many farm children. This was not the case with Lizzie. She knew how hard she had struggled and begged Delcy for a chance to read and write. Education for Mary Antionette and Frank Robert became an obsession with Lizzie. She had taught Frank

Robert and Mary Antionette as much as she could with the limited education she was able to acquire from Miss Liza.

Frank Robert and Mary Antionette were very bright students. They both were able to read, write and do math when they entered school. Every morning Lizzie would hook up the team of mules to the wagon and drive the four miles to Nicholasville for Frank Robert and Mary Antionette to go to school. At the appropriate time Mary Antoinette graduated from high school and enrolled in Kentucky State Teachers College, Frankfort, Kentucky, a Land Grant College for "colored" students. The program offered a two-year certificate in teaching. Frank Robert followed behind two years later and enrolled in a teacher education program with an interest in History. Mary Antionette graduated with her two-year certificate in 1934. She was hired to teach at Little Zion, the country school she had once attended as a child in Jessamine County.

It was during her tenure as a teacher that she met a tiny little girl named Katherine Louise Black who she befriended. Louise would come to Little Zion with her brother Robert so she would not be left alone while her mother and father worked as sharecroppers on a nearby farm. Louise was often alone and Mary Antionette knew this. One cold snowy day, Mary Antionette asked Katie, Louise's mother, permission for Louise to come and live with them. Katie gave permission for Louise to be in the loving care of Lizzie. It was easy for her to serve as a foster mother to Louise.

When Mary Antionette left Kentucky and moved to Hampton, Virginia to complete her four years of college, she met her husband

Richard Patrick and never returned to Kentucky to live. Louise remained in the loving care of Lizzie and Simon. Frank Robert continued his education at Kentucky State Teachers College where he met his wife Ora Belle Hamilton. After graduating with a certificate in History, Frank Robert and Ora Belle were married in May 1936. After the marriage of Frank Robert and Ora Belle they moved to Nicholasville and assumed residence with Lizzie and Simon.

Frank Robert began his teaching career at the Jessamine County School for Colored Children under the principalship of Professor Julius Caesar Caldwell, where he once attended as a boy.

Lizzie was very wise, and yet soft and gentle, loved, and gave so much love. She quietly died in her sleep at the age of ninety-four on September 8, 1965.

EPILOGUE

In the summer of 1938, June 27, I began my journey with Mama, my grandmother, Lizzie. No, there was no slave ship on the shores of West Africa waiting at anchor to begin its voyage to America. There was no slave master waiting to auction my body to the highest bidder, nor divide the family into separate pieces of property so one's roots could never be connected again. I am humbled by the past stories that were told to Mama by her mother Delcy. It is a privilege to walk in the footprints of Mama as she revealed her stories to me, her granddaughter.

Mama was a tiny grandmother, barely five feet tall and weighing less than one hundred pounds. She had long white hair that was worn in a small bun on the back of her head and a wave of hair that draped her forehead. Her voice was soft, warm and tender. I rarely ever heard her raise her voice even to laugh out loud. I never remember Mama being young. When I was born, Mama was sixty-eight years old. She began sharing her stories and life struggles with me when she was in her seventies. I vividly remember her little round wire rim glasses and false teeth that she would take out every night and put in a case on the night stand beside her bed. Mama always wore long cotton print dresses and aprons made from feed sacks. Her underclothes were all homemade from bleached white feed sacks. Her petticoat was as long as her dress and her underwear, called teddies, were simple and accommodating. Mama always wore brown or black cotton stockings and brown, laced shoes representing the simplicity of her life.

Many of the stories she told reflected the spiritual and religious values that she instilled in her children and grandchildren. If one listened closely while she was washing clothes or preparing dinner, one would hear her singing her favorite hymn from the old brown covered Gospel Pearl Songbook, published by the Sunday School Evangelistic Meeting Convention, Nashville, Tennessee, 1921.

"Marching homeward day by day, To a land that's free from weeping. Singing all along the way, Of the Savior and His love. Trusting in Him day and night, Sweetly resting in his keeping and for right we will fight, Till we're safe with Him above."

The more she sang the song, the more I would be drawn into the words and what they must have meant to her through her journey to freedom. As I grew older, the songs Mama used to sing and the stories she told took on a new meaning and substance.

We shared a bedroom for eighteen years before I left home to enter college at what is now Kentucky State University in Frankfort, Kentucky. Our tiny bedroom included two windows in the room, one facing east and one facing south, that gave Mama and me a beautiful view of the farm. When the weather was clear the two of us could see for miles. On the wall were two family pictures going back to the days of slavery. One was a very large framed picture of Mama's mother, Delcy, and the other was a smaller framed picture of her mother's sister, Mary Brent. The pictures had very stern facial expressions with deep piercing eyes. Sometimes their expressions were so frightening that I would hide under the cover to keep from looking at them. One time I asked Mama why they looked so angry. Mama replied,

"They didn't have much to smile about, being a slave working from sunup until sundown. They never knew from day to day if they would have enough food to eat or if they would be sold and separated from their children, family and friends".

I cherished sleeping in the little twin bed next to Mama. There was a sense of security when the storms would rage outside with the winds and rain dashing against the window. Mama would gently pat her hand on the side of the bed beckoning for me to crawl into her bed, where she would gently cradle me in her arms and sing the old spiritual, Stand By Me.

"When the storms of life are raging, stand by me. When the world is tossing me like a ship upon the sea, Thou who rules wind and water, stand by me."

Mama's bed was always comforting and neatly adorned with fluffy hand pieced quilts. One night I asked her to tell me about the beautiful star quilt on her bed. As she told the story about the Northern Star Quilt, she said,

"The star was designed to guide the escaping slaves into the northern cities on their way to Canada. Some called the quilt the Ohio Star because Ohio was a free state, and many escaping slaves were sometimes guided by the star quilt to reach the free state of Ohio. So when the Northern Star quilt was displayed in Ohio on rail fences or near a safe house that protected fugitive slaves, the fleeing slaves knew they were headed north."

The story fascinated me so much that I asked about the quilt on my bed. It was heavy and warm. Mama explained that it was a nine patch square quilt made from the scraps of many old dresses, shirts and aprons that had a few good spots left in them. She explained how the nine patches were used to write the names of family members who no longer worked or lived on the same plantation. Their names and sometimes birth dates were scribbled on the square and saved as a record of family members. Mama said that the families always hoped that they would meet again someday, and the quilt would be a reminder of who was born and was once a part of the family. Unfortunately, many families that were separated during slavery, as well as during the Civil War, never returned to the plantations to join their loved ones.

I was always curious about the old rusty round top trunk that was in a dark corner of the attic. Sometimes I would sneak into the attic searching for old memories that were a part of the past. Most of the time I was scared to enter the dark room because I could hardly find my way due to a lot of junk things. I wondered if there were other old quilts stored in the trunk that had history pertinent to the Underground Railroad in Kentucky. With that in mind, I began to search from room to room in the big house looking for all kinds of quilt patterns. All the family members that lived in the big house had quilts on their beds.

The flying geese quilt was one of Mama's favorites. From time to time I asked Mama about the quilts in the trunk. I really wanted Mama to tell me about her favorite quilt. She began one afternoon to tell me her story as the seasons were beginning to change from summer to fall, and the air had a certain chill that was a reminder that cold weather was near. As Mama and I sat outside on the old rusty swing that hung from the ceiling beams of the front porch, Mama was very quiet. We sat together on the swing many times talking and folding clothes or quilting and sometimes visiting with family and friends. This particular afternoon was different because Mama wanted me to listen and be quiet. I asked her,

"What were we listening for?"

She replied, "The sounds of fall."

Way up in the sky we could hear the Canadian Geese "honking" as they flew in a perfect V over the house. What a strange sound. The geese were flying south for the fall and winter where they would find food and water. In the spring they would return north when the rivers and streams would be thawed from the cold winter months. Finally, the beautiful quilt story was revealed. Mama really cherished the special flying geese quilt. She said that most slaves escaping north relied on the hidden messages in certain quilts to alert them that the Underground Railroad that followed the rivers and lakes north was now open.

I looked on all the beds for the flying geese quilt. I could not find it on any of the eight beds occupied by the family members. I asked Mama to show me the flying geese quilt that was in the attic in the big trunk. I really wanted to know why it was so important to Mama and the family. After a few days, Mama decided it was time to share what was in the old trunk. She got an old oil lamp and carefully lit it. She beckoned for me to follow her up stairs to the dark attic for a look in the old trunk. It was dark in there. We would hear the sound of mice scurrying across the floor trying to hide behind some of the old boxes and clothes that cluttered the attic. I was not afraid as long as Mama was ahead of me with the old lamp. She cautioned me to never try to bring a lighted candle or lamp into the attic because I could cause a fire and that would destroy the home and others may get hurt. I never will forget the lesson on safety as we entered the dark attic room.

After opening the old trunk in the attic, there was the flying geese quilt neatly folded among other beautiful quilts and lace edged sheets and hand embroidered pillowcases. I thought every thing in the old trunk was absolutely beautiful. Mama gently opened the quilt and looked at all the beautiful pieces that were lined up side-by-side forming a perfect "V". When I asked about other quilts in the trunk, Mama assured me that some were her mother's and others were family favorites. I asked Mama how she knew so much about the quilts and their patterns. She replied, "Delcy, your great grandmother, told me the secrets of the quilts that her mother, my grandmother Leah, had told her."

The secrets of the quilt patterns were entrusted to the family members as a legacy to the freedom of slaves as they traveled the Underground Railroad. Mama replied that she had given as a wedding gift some of the family quilts to her daughter Mary Antionette who lived in Lynchburg, Virginia.

The family home on Nicholasville road, about six miles south of Lexington, was a friendly place for many people. It was located on US Highway 27 and was convenient for friends to drop in for a visit.

Visitors were always welcomed with open arms and offered something to eat. For example, the old Watkins salesman was always peddling his ointments, salves, vanilla and spices to the farmers in the area. Apparently, he managed to time his visit with Mama when the family was having breakfast. He always started out by telling Mama how good everything smelled. I often wondered if he actually smelled the bacon and sausage cooking as he pulled in the drive in his horse drawn buggy, or if he just felt welcome sitting at the family table eating breakfast. Whichever the case, Mama would have never turned him away. Like the Watkins salesman, there were numerous hobos who would stop for milk and bread. There always seemed to be plenty to go around for the family and to share with others. One of the sweet spirits of Mama was her willingness to share. She would say,

"It makes my heart sing with joy, and sing I must do for Christ's sake. He is the one that gives me all I have and I know how easy it is to lose all you have."

Mama continued to give and share with others and trust that God would always supply her needs; He truly did.

During the summer, I was very busy helping Mama pick the fruit from the orchard and gather the vegetables from the garden. Summer was a big time on the farm. Sometimes Mama would can over a thousand jars of fruits and vegetables in preparation for the winter months. Mama would kill the oldest ducks and chickens for meat, and my job was to help pluck the feathers, especially from the ducks, to be used to stuff fresh pillows and mattresses for the winter. Those old feather-tic mattresses were big and lumpy and hard to make up in the morning before going to school.

Among Mama's prized possessions was the big old family Bible that was once her mother's. I was always curious about the large family Bible dating back to 1876. There was a special place in the living room that one could always find the Bible. The children were not allowed to play in the living room. It was set aside for guests and visitors. There were French doors that separated the living room from the family room where I spent most of my younger days. On special occasions, and with permission, Mama would share the beautiful pictures of her family and the history of all the births, deaths, and marriages of the Brent, Smith, and Cannon families. So many had died young. Mama would talk about the family and the hardship of seeing the children die at a young age. On the wall in the living room were two very special pictures of family members. I thought it was strange that no other pictures were displayed in that room.

One day, I asked Mama to tell me about the pictures. She told me that one picture was of her three sons by Simon; the other, was his portrait. She spoke of her sorrow at the death of the three sons and how Simon was special. Because of his love for her and the children, he provided them a home for life.

Sometimes Mama would tell stories about the lives of her family as they struggled through slavery. She often recalled the hardships of her family as they journeyed toward freedom. Once Mama told me to,

"Get a good education and study hard."

She never forgot how difficult it was for her to learn to read and write while helping with the chores on the plantation. She always stressed getting an education and studying. I can remember her faithfully reading the Bible and a daily prayer guide called "The Upper Room." Mama was a dedicated Church member, both financially and spiritually, and she made sure everyone in the family went to church every Sunday. She was very faithful in preparing the unleavened bread for the Communion Sunday service. She would carefully make the salt-free pastry and lightly bake the bread. Afterward, she would prepare the grape juice that was poured into little tiny communion cups and placed in shiny silver trays. I looked forward to the first Sunday in each month when Mama would help the preacher serve communion to the congregation. After the service, Mama would allow all the children to eat the left over bread and empty the little glass communion cups. The memory of the things that Mama did for me made a great impression on my life.

I vividly remember the times when Mama would visit her brothers and sisters who resided in Leesburg, Kentucky. The family gatherings were celebrated at the Methodist Church in Leesburg where Mama's parents, brothers, and sisters are buried. The little country church was surrounded by thick brush, weeds, and an out door toilet. I was always afraid of finding field mice and especially snakes in the churchyard. Whatever the fear may have been, there were no excuses to not attend the basket meeting at the church. Each family member would bring covered dishes of food to serve and share with the others. This celebration called "basket meeting" was held once a year usually in

July. It was always hot and there were plenty ants, bugs, and mosquitoes. I was always glad when the family gathering was over, because I had severe allergies and the weeds and chiggers made for a miserable day. However, I knew this was a special time for Mama to be with her family, and as a result, I tried to never show any displeasure in going to the reunion out of respect for Mama.

Among the fondest memories I have of Mama are the old fashioned recipes she used to prepare for the family. Her white bean soup with ham and cornbread was something worth waiting for. Mama taught me to cook most of the foods for the family by watching and helping her. Another one of Mama's favorite recipes was fried fruit pie. This recipe was never written down, but I know her mother passed it on to her. Mama would use fruit from the orchard that was dried by slicing it into quarters and spreading it on top of an old tin roof that covered the chicken house to dry. My job was to spread the apples, peaches, and apricots on the hot tin roof in the morning, then gather them all up in the evening before sunset. If the evening dew were to dampen the fruit, this would cause it to mold and spoil. The drying process took about a week. After the fruit was thoroughly dry, Mama would put it in clean feed sacks to be stored in a cool place until she was ready to make her special fried fruit pies.

Mama was also an expert at making "home brewed beer". In the cellar of the house was a dark, dead end room that was used for storing the special "home brew beer". I was never given the recipe but as much as my memory serves, the ingredients included: yeast, malt, sugar, water and hops. Mama would mix all the ingredients in a big crock jug, covering it tightly to allow the brew to ferment and turn into beer. After a designated time, she would pour the beer into dark colored bottles, tightly pressing corks in the top of each and placing them in the dark room. After a few weeks, when the house was very quiet, one could hear the corks popping and the beer spewing everywhere. This meant that the home brew was ready to be served.

Mama would say to the children,

"Stay out of the cellar, there's a big black snake hiding under the steps."

She knew it was tempting to the grandchildren to sneak down stairs to taste the "home brew beer." Mama would always invite grown-folks to have a bottle of the special brew. Visitors and friends of Mama seemed to come back year after year waiting for her to invite them to have a bottle or two.

One Sunday, the preacher was invited to dinner with the family. After eating, the preacher asked Mama if he could have a little of that special brew. Mama replied,

"I suppose so, a little never hurt anyone."

We watched the preacher drink one, then two, and then three bottles. When he got ready to get out of his chair to leave he was as "drunk as a skunk" as we would say in the south. I laughed and laughed. Poor old Reverend, he tried to walk but his legs were like rubber. All he could do was sink back in the chair and laugh too.

We soon found out just how sick the "home brew" would make us feel. Once my younger brother decided to sneak a few bottles out of the basement without Mama's knowledge. He drank the warm brew "like a man." Sure enough, after about an hour, my little brother was crawling in the house "sick as a dog." I knew that the home brew had done a number on him.

Now I know why Mama always told the children it would make us sick if we drank it. I used to shake the bottle, then pop the cork and sip the rich white foam as it ran down the bottle. I wished I had never tried the warm bottle of brew. "Too much, too late."

I'm sure everyone has a homemade remedy story. Mama's mother, Delcy, shared her recipe as far back as 1885. Mama would cook a special root tea in the spring of the year that everyone in the family had to drink including the children. The tea was made from roots that she would gather from the field and around tree trunks. She would combine the roots in a big pot filled with water and place it on the back of the wood burning stove. It would seemingly simmer for days. It smelled terrible. When the water would boil low, Mama would add a little more and continue steaming the roots. When it was ready, it was as dark as bark on a tree. Mama would line up all the children and give each one a big cup to drink. It tasted terrible, even after you added lots of sugar. When I asked Mama,

"Why do we have to drink the dark root tea?" Mama replied,

"It will kill all the winter germs and make you healthy for the summer."

Mama had a reason and answer for everything. After our share, the adults would have some. No one ever dared not to drink their share, and there was always more where that came from. In retrospect, we were really healthy and rarely had bad colds. I never knew the ingredients used in this tea and cannot imagine finding the right combination of herbs to duplicate the recipe.

I inherited the old pecan rocking chair that dates back to 1850 when Mama's grandparents, Eli and Leah Brent, were sold into slavery to work on the Sheff tobacco plantation in Leesburg, Kentucky. The rocker was one of a few pieces of furniture found in the old log cabin placed there by Master Lloyd. I have since had the old rocker restored to its original pattern. One childhood memory of the old chair was that it had little short rockers and was very low to the floor. If one rocked back too far, it would tip over. Today, it sits in my bedroom alongside the original dresser that Mama and I shared in the big farmhouse on the hill. Mama shared her final stories at the age of 94. She commented that,

"God left me here for a reason. I was the first child born to Delcy in 1870 and I will be the last child to die. I have lived a long time, a life full of sorrow and joy. Love each other as I have loved each of you."

Over the years there was one story that Mama never shared with me, but my father, Frank Robert, did. Before his death May 8, 1988, my father shared the story of how Delcy, Mama's mother, was brutally beaten and raped by Lloyd Sheff for "sassy" and intolerable behavior. Delcy never forgave him for the harsh treatment. Before leaving the plantation, Delcy crushed broken glass so fine that it looked like powder and daily stirred a few teaspoons of the glass into Lloyd Sheff's buttermilk. Over a period of a few months, Lloyd began to bleed from the bowels. The disease was diagnosed as the "flux".

Little did the Sheff family know at that time that Delcy was keeping her vow that Lloyd Sheff would never beat or violate her sexually again. Lloyd Sheff died in the year 1880 prior to the family leaving the plantation. Delcy never forgave nor forgot the rape she encountered at the hands of Lloyd Sheff that resulted in her pregnancy and the birth of Mama Lizzie. Although Mama was conceived of violence, her life exemplified love that she demonstrated in many ways throughout her life.

Mama died in her sleep on September 8, 1965.

Chronology of Events

1850	Eli, Leah, Reuben and Josh arrive in America at the Annapolis, Maryland slave market.
1854	Delcy Brent, daughter of Eli and Leah Brent, is born November 18, 1854; died April 6, 1926
1854	Neut Smith, sharecropper on Lloyd Sheff plantation, born September 10, 1854; died October 30, 1916
1870	Lizzie Brent Sheff, daughter of Delcy and Master Lloyd Sheff, born December 25, 1870
1871	Neut and Delcy marry in the spring of 1871. To this union 13 children are born.
1870 – 1880	Lizzie lives on Sheff plantation with Mama Delcy, Neut, and siblings.
1880	Lizzie leaves the plantation with parents and siblings and moves to the Walter's farm in Georgetown, Kentucky.
1887	Lizzie meets Jim Davis at a church gathering in Leesburg, Kentucky. They are married in the spring of 1887. Three children are born to this union: William Aaron (July 26, 1888), Leah Ann (March 1, 1891) and Charlie (June 8, 1893).
1895	Jim and Lizzie divorce
1898	Lizzie marries Simon Cannon, November 12, 1898. To this union five children are born: Elmer (May 15, 1900), Joe (January 13, 1902), Roy (July 30, 1904),

Mary Antionette (March 10, 1911), and Frank Robert (August 8, 1913). Two other children complete the family: Annie Bell (March 1, 1896), Simon's daughter by a previous marriage, and Katherine Louise Black (January 21, 1926), Lizzie's foster daughter.

1936	Frank Robert marries Ora Belle Hamilton. To this union three children are born: Frank Robert, Jr. (February 10, 1937), Mary Clarice (June 27, 1938) and John Merrell (May 17, 1939).
1965	Lizzie Brent Sheff Davis Cannon dies.
1988	Frank Robert, Sr. dies.
2001	Mary Clarice Cannon Boswell writes the story of her family's history from slavery to freedom.

Author Information

Dr. Clarice Boswell has resided in the Joliet, Illinois vicinity with her husband Hank since 1959. She is the mother of four children and has seven grandchildren. Dr. Boswell received her early training in Nicholasville, Kentucky where her father was principal of the colored school. She attended Kentucky State College, a land grant historically black college, where she received a bachelor degree in nutrition and home economics education and met her husband, Hank.

After moving to Joliet, Illinois in 1959, Mrs. Boswell worked as a dietitian at Silver Cross Hospital before being employed at Joliet East High School as a home economics teacher. In 1962 Mrs. Boswell entered Northern Illinois University where she earned a master's degree in education while simultaneously working on a second master's degree from Illinois State University in counseling with an emphasis on pupil personnel services.

In the fall of 1968, Mrs. Boswell was assigned to the counseling department at Joliet East High School where she served until it closed in 1984. She transferred to Joliet West High School as a counselor and career education advisor. In the fall of 1988, Mrs. Boswell re-entered Northern Illinois University to pursue a doctorate degree in adult continuing education with a focus on leadership, education, policies and service. Dr. Boswell graduated in May 1991 with her Ed. D degree. In the fall of 1990, Dr. Boswell was selected to chair the department of pupil personnel services at Joliet Central High School where she served for five years before retiring in June of 1995.

Dr. Boswell was so impressed with the historical research defining the struggle of historically black institutions that she continued her research to include the origin, struggle and journey of her family.

Delcy Brent Smith, born, November 18, 1854 to Leah and Eli Brent. Married Neut Smith, Spring 1871. To this union thirteen children were born. Delcy died April 6, 1926 in Leesburg, Kentucky.

Lizzie Brent Sheff Davis, age 28.

Lizzie Brent Sheff Davis Cannon, born December 25, 1870, was the mother of eight children and one foster daughter, Katherine Louise Black, whom she raised from the age of five. At Lizzie's death on September 8, 1965, at the age of 94, she had nine grandchildren and four children living that lovingly called her Mama.

Simon Cannon, born, March 1, 1872. The second husband of Lizzie and the father of Anna Bell and five children with Lizzie.

Neut Smith, born September 10, 1854, Moved to Kentucky looking for work in 1870. He stopped at the Sheff plantation where he was hired as a tobacco sharecropper for the Lloyd Sheff family. There he met Delcy (and baby Lizzie) who worked for the Sheff family. After a short courtship, Delcy and Neut were married in the spring of 1871. To this union, thirteen children were born.

House on the hill in Nicholasville, Kentucky that Simon Cannon built for his wife Lizzie and their children in 1917. Remodeled porch and siding added.

The tobacco fields of Kentucky were rich and fertile. The crops of Burley tobacco were tended by slaves with overseers that were often harsh and cruel. Sometimes food and water were withheld from the slaves as a punishment for not working as fast as the Master thought they should.

The old log cabin on the farm purchased by Simon Cannon, Leah and Frank Strauss, and Charlie Davis. Later, in 1935, Frank Cannon inherited Simon's share; William Davis bought out his brother Charlie, and Leah and Frank Strauss lived in the old log cabin. It still remains on the farm owned by the Cannon family. 2001.

African Methodist Church–

Leesburg, Kentucky

1927

CPSIA information can be obtained
at www.ICGtesting.com
Printed in the USA
JSHW032150070423
40046JS00006B/23

9 780759 699205